"I met Jack in 1992 when I had been traded from the Cincinnati Reds to the New York Yankees. It is no coincidence my best years in baseball were in New York. Jack helped me change my career and life and helped me realize how my faith could drive me on and off the field."

—**Paul O'Neill**, Former All-Star Outfielder and American League Batting Champion for the New York Yankees

"As a corporate executive, I think this book will have a significant impact on young corporate leaders. It fills a void in corporate life."

—**Mitchell Modell**, Modell Sporting Goods Chairman, CEO, and President

"As a lawyer and entrepreneur, and having known Jack for many years, I have witnessed his commonsense approach to life and business. He has touched the lives of so many people both professionally and personally. The ideas in this book are very special."

—**Randall Bentley**, Partner, Bentley, Bentley, and Bentley

"I have been honored to know Jack for nearly 25 years. I have seen him improve the performances of hundreds of athletes from the ranks of amateurs to the professional elite. During this time he has also mentored me in various aspects of my business life. I cannot count how many times I have walked away from a conversation with Jack, gaining a commonsense solution to a business challenge. The challenges of his clients pale in comparison the Jack's personal challenges with adversity. His commonsense approach to leadership is refreshing, entertaining, and very effective."

—**Chet Burke**, Chairman, Chet Burke Productions

"I have worked with Jack since the late 70's on both business and sport projects. As owner of a sport organization which spans 32 countries, I have found an ever increasing lack of commonsense in resolving complex issues. This book has been needed for a very long time. I look forward to making it available to our administrators in all 32 countries."

—**Donald Ruedlinger**, Chairman and CEO Youth Basketball of America

COMMONSENSE
LEADERSHIP

COMMONSENSE LEADERSHIP

No-Nonsense Rules
FOR IMPROVING YOUR
MENTAL GAME
AND INCREASING YOUR
Team's Performance

JACK H. LLEWELLYN

WILEY

ISBN 978-1-119-28782-7 (cloth)
ISBN 978-1-119-28783-4 (ePDF)
ISBN 978-1-119-28784-1 (ePub)

Printed in the United States of America

10 9 8 7 6 5 4 3 2 1

This book presented a major challenge for me.
Facing cognitive issues with my multiple sclerosis (MS),
I am so appreciative
of two friends and colleagues for helping me.
With this in mind, I dedicate this book to Danny Gershwin,
who transcribed the manuscript. He is a special friend
who pushed me to get it done.
I also appreciate my loyal friend, Chet Burke,
who is always an inspiration to me on
all my projects and shares my commonsense perspective toward
dealing with both business issues and my personal challenges with MS.
My son Tripp was very instrumental in helping me focus every day.
I also dedicate the book to my three other children:
Hunter, Tate, and Abbott. They helped me keep my focus
on commonsense solutions to seemingly complex issues.

Contents

Foreword

Anyone in a leadership role today has likely been exposed to some form of leadership training—be that classes, mentors, books, or remote courses. All of those have a place in leadership development. Yet rarely do you find a resource that combines the best of these various types of learning in a truly engaging format. In this book, Dr. Jack Llewellyn does just that. He taps into the critical importance of an individual leader understanding the internal mental game, as well as how that leader can use this to increase team performance.

I've known Dr. Jack for over 15 years. I have come to know him personally and professionally. During that time, he has successfully shared his leadership and life lessons with me, with several of my financial services management and sales teams, and with my wife's pharmaceutical management teams. No matter the industry, he is able to connect very common sense principles to the specific situation of the audience. He continues this connectivity in this latest book.

I met Dr. Jack at a national sales meeting for Prudential Retirement where he was our featured speaker. At the time, I was managing a team of 25 retirement sales professionals. I began using his "assets and liabilities" approach not only for myself but for our team as well. His research, commentary, and mentorship helped me become a more focused and meaningful leader. My interactions with him, whether at a national sales meeting, individually, or over the phone, are always positive and humorous. There are so many daily challenges that we all face as leaders, and it is so important to remain positive—no matter what the obstacle.

Since we have all read many leadership books, it is important to state that there is a certain magic to how Dr. Jack presents his concepts. He is very skilled at taking common, everyday life examples to illustrate his leadership principles. From his work as a sports psychologist, he overflows with stories of how individuals and teams can thrive when great leaders are present. Basically, he has lived through all of these principles as a life coach. He is expert in helping leaders in any industry—from sports to corporate boardrooms—tap into the mental aspect of high performing teams.

I am very confident that if you are in a leadership role of any kind—community, organization, corporation—that clearly you will be enriched and will benefit from *Commonsense Leadership*.

Greg Poplarski, AIF, RPA, PRP
Director, Retirement Specialist
Allianz Investors

Preface

Who are you today and who do you want to be tomorrow? This is a question that you need to answer every day for both your professional and personal life. Even though leadership is the focus of this book, it is virtually impossible to be a leader until you conduct a thorough self-examination. Instead of having others define you with the theoretical stuff of leadership books or seminars, you need to define yourself.

Looking at most leadership guides today, it's easy to get so obsessed with counting things that we lose track of commonsense answers. What are the seven habits of leaders? What are the 14 tips for winning? I don't know the answer to either question. Structured theories like these rob people of their identifying characteristics. You must use a commonsense approach to every day, both professionally and personally, to determine who you are and what works for you.

If you want to be a leader, first define what a leader does and how a leader is defined by colleagues. We typically define leaders by position or title, but this is misguided. I think that the majority of CEOs, CFOs, COOs, and chairpersons are not leaders. They are coaches and managers who create environments in which leaders can lead.

Leaders are most often team members, and some of them are even reluctant to lead. They lead through performance. Remember the old adage "What you do speaks so loudly people can't hear what you say." The most effective leaders understand this and lead by example. Others try too hard to be leaders and end up seeming like all talk.

I worked with a major-league baseball player a few years ago who was really struggling with his on-field performance. He was very talented offensively and defensively, but he wasn't able to channel any of his skill on game day. The general manager called me, a sports-psychology consultant, because the team was concerned about the player's performance.

I called the player and asked him a critical question: "How do you want to be perceived on the team?"

His response was that he wanted to be a team leader.

My next question was, "How do you lead?"

His answer was, "I talk with players, try to get them pumped up."

That was the source of his struggles. Instead of talking, he needed to act as a leader through his performance. To do that, he had to play the game with emotional intensity every day and let his skills, passion, and behavior send a message. We talked several times a week and his performance picked up. In fact, he went on to win the Silver Slugger Award, which is given to the top hitter in each field position, and he made the All-Star team. More importantly, his team began to see him as a leader, and he has kept that important role every season since we had our initial phone call.

In another case, I worked with a player who was a classic reluctant leader. In fact, he was committed to *not* taking on a leadership role. Despite this player's reservations, his character, work ethic, and talent ensured that he became the leader—and he will always hold a prominent place in his team's history.

The bottom line is that leaders come in many forms. We often talk about natural leaders, people born with the talent and personality traits to blossom when given a positive environment. The fact of the matter is, great leaders are not born, they are *made*, whether it happens on a ball field or in a conference room.

This book provides commonsense solutions to issues often perceived as major problems in the corporate environment. Too often we muddy the water by combining coaching and training, neglecting the difference between these two activities. *Training* is teaching work skills. It usually focuses on processes, procedures, tools, and technology. *Coaching* is harnessing those skills to best fit the work environment. Coaches create an environment in which leaders can lead. It's about putting skills in context—the key to cultivating a strong leadership at every level of your organization. In short, leadership is *learned*. It emerges through trial and error, which is made easier when you adhere to commonsense approaches to the work process.

This book guides potential leaders through the process of self-evaluation to determine if they have the tools to succeed. If you decide to become a leader, then you are supported through a process to develop the necessary skills.

Remember, it takes more than a title to make a leader. True leaders are defined by their performance and by how they touch people's lives every day.

Chapter 1

Let Common Sense Be Your Guide to Leading

I was invited to speak at an international life-coaching convention a few years ago, and asked the person who had contacted me by phone, "What do you do?"

She said, "We certify corporate coaches and life coaches."

I was curious so I asked her, "What do you personally do?"

She said, "I'm a certified life and corporate coach."

Her voice and enthusiasm had given me the impression that she was quite young, so I asked her how old she was. "I'm 21," she said.

That fact alone gave me some reservations about this young woman's organization. After all, experience—both in the workplace and life in general—is crucial to coaching. Before declining, I decided to get a second opinion. I called a friend of mine who was a corporate executive and I asked, "What are some criteria you use to hire life coaches and corporate coaches?"

He laughed and he said, "Their hair has to be grayer than mine."

That made the decision for me. There are so many organizations that make money off coaching certification programs without setting clear standards for the people they claim to serve. They plant an idea in the minds of these young people, leading them to believe they can be successful when they're not really qualified to coach. That's not to say that someday they won't have enough experience under their belts to be effective coaches, but certifying recent college grads who have spent limited time in any professional situation sends the wrong message about what coaching entails.

I think leadership falls into that same category. There are obviously many types of leadership: the inherited leadership, especially in family-owned businesses; corporate leadership, where board members talk about who is next in line to be CEO or chairman; and there are top performers, especially in sales where it's easy to set up a leaderboard and compare numbers. In most cases when we talk about leadership, we're thinking about people in the context of being the next leaders of the company. But this perspective has some serious drawbacks.

For example, many times in sales-oriented companies it can really hurt the sales force when the person with the best sales numbers is promoted to a management position. I've known a lot of salespeople who have told me that they hope they don't get promoted to sales manager because they love selling. Well, the next thing you, know they're promoted to manager and don't sell anymore. The problem is they're not management people—not *coaches*. As salespeople, they may have shown true leadership and carried themselves in such a way that it motivated other people. Top-performing salespeople have a few things in common: They talk to people. They consult with their colleagues. They create a positive environment for sales. But when you make those people managers, you take them out of the sales force, which hurts the company in two ways. First, they are no longer in a position where they sell well, stay happy, and naturally emerge as leaders. Second, they are unhappy and often ill equipped to manage the team.

It's always been my rule of thumb to tell people in the corporate world that it's up to the executives to create an environment and *let the leaders lead*.

One night at midnight my phone rang. The caller was a general manager of a Major League Baseball team; it was the first time in 45 years I had been called by a general manager. Between that and the late hour, I figured his team must be working through something pretty serious. He said, "We have a great kid. I really like him, he's struggling. He needs to talk to you."

I said, "Well, I will call him first thing in the morning."

The general manager said, "No, he'll be in his room at 12:15."

So I called him just after midnight and we talked till 2:00 AM. The issue was that he wanted to be a leader on the team. He was a verbal person and he talked a lot to players. He also spent a lot of time trying to motivate other people, which, unfortunately, often involved him yelling at them.

My point was very simple. I said, "Leaders show leadership through performance. If you go out and be who you are and play the best you can play every single day and do what *you* can do every single day to help the team win, you're going to be recognized as the leader." It was another matter of actions speaking louder than words.

Well, the next year he won the Silver Slugger Award and made the All-Star team. Just as important to him, he was considered a leader on the team. His teammates noticed his hard work and began to look to him for motivation. But then the team let him get away as a free agent, which left them with no leadership at all.

I've always thought it's interesting to watch a team perform after the leaders are gone. That's when you have so many people trying to establish themselves as a leader, which can sometimes be a very, very negative direction.

I worked with one corporation at three different levels of management: sales, middle management, and executive. It was an interesting environment because it was a growing company, there was a lot of room for growth, and they tried to promote from within. During my time working with the company, I had many meetings with salespeople and several of them asked me, "Can you talk to the vice president for sales and tell him not to promote me to regional sales manager?"

3

In a lot of different corporate environments, we get so obsessed with performance numbers that we don't look beyond those when considering leadership positions. Your best leaders may not be your top performers but rather the people who enable top performers to achieve high levels. You can detect this in a number of ways, but none of them are as easy as tracking sales data.

Leaders need to be especially involved with the development of *chemistry* in the corporate environment. This intangible factor is often overlooked by those who are involved with numbers or obsessed with profit. I have seen firsthand, both in the corporate environment and in sports environments, that chemistry is one of those things that you never miss until it's gone.

Many years ago I worked with a team that was on a ten-game winning streak and a reporter asked one of the athletes, "To what do you attribute this streak?"

He said, "It's because we've been playing well, we hit the ball well, we score a lot of runs."

"What about chemistry?" the reporter asked.

And the athlete said, "Chemistry is way overplayed. That's just something people like to talk about."

Well, about a month later we went on an eight-game losing streak. The same athlete faced the same reporter, who asked, "To what do you attribute the losing streak?"

"Well," the player said, "I don't know. Man, we've lost our chemistry."

Chemistry, that abstract element that maintains synergy and keeps things running well, is something we don't talk about a lot, but it has everything to do with team performance. As in the sports world, if we don't operate as a team in the corporate world, then we're just developing individual performers. Even if they do everything they can, we as an organization will never reach the levels we need to reach because it's impossible for individuals to get there on their own.

Everybody needs to be a part of a team—and leaders are the ones who help people recognize that.

We'll talk about chemistry and a positive work environment in Chapter 7. All you need to know right now is that if you have a negative environment, you're not going to succeed, no matter what kind of talent you have. However, if you have a positive environment, you increase your probability for success because you'll have the right chemistry keeping things together.

Everything I talk about in this book hinges on the fact that talent overrides everything else. I don't care how good you feel about your leadership qualities. If you don't have talent, you can't play. It's a hard fact. I've been in corporate environments where people with the talent to talk and schmooze the right people have, in fact, been promoted up through companies, but they weren't successful over the long term as executives because they didn't have the talent to play.

The first thing that you need to examine if you have aspirations of being a leader is that it takes not only knowledge but also time, communication skills, and personality traits—all of which lend themselves to leadership. You need to decide who you want to be and what you want to do with your life, both in the corporate environment and personally. Too many times leaders are people who have been assigned a label, but they're not true leaders in the corporate environment. The true leaders, as I said before, are within the workforce, in every department. Leaders are very team oriented, but they can also make decisions. They are the people who are recognized—often by their peers—for what they do to help the group succeed.

One thing to be careful of, if you are an aspiring leader, is to examine your personality to ensure you have the traits necessary to succeed in a leadership position. Some people, no matter how badly they want to be in charge, are not cut out to be true leaders who inspire those around them. As for people who are natural followers, that's fine, too. You don't have to be a leader to be successful. Some people are at their best when they are part of a supportive environment but do not have to make key decisions.

Chapter 3 is devoted to the subject of personality, something that you don't see in many leadership books. Most of the industry relies on tests and evaluations to determine who should be given a leader label, but these methods are often superficial and I don't think they help us get a read on who people really are. This sets unattainable expectations because we want a person to become someone who matches the label we've assigned. That doesn't often work out.

For example, I spoke at a corporate environment where, before I arrived, the organizers had given a personality inventory and categorized people into four boxes. I don't recall what the boxes were exactly—introverts, extroverts, leaders, and followers—but they assigned each personality type a color (red, yellow, green, and blue). Then, they bought T-shirts in the colors of the four categories for the conference attendees to wear. This was meant to facilitate better communication in the company.

When I arrived at the meeting, everybody was wearing a T-shirt in one of the four identifying colors. The interesting thing to me was the fact that all the yellow shirts sat in one section, all green shirts in another, and so on. Instead of improving communication, they had pigeonholed people into categories. It turned out that everyone felt more comfortable talking to the people wearing the same color T-shirt.

There are many tests that categorize people into different slots, but I don't think they are fair and I think you lose some potential leaders in the process. You stifle the productivity of a company and shut down individual creativity. Even worse, you establish a relationship dynamic instead of letting one emerge through natural chemistry.

Unlike other leadership guides, this book is based on experience and observation instead of theory. In my 45 years of experience as a sports psychologist and consultant, I have talked to people at every level in both the corporate and athletics worlds. It might surprise you that the leadership skills in those two arenas are not very different.

Some of the greatest athletes I've ever worked with were some of the worst leaders that I've ever been around. Many times you can look at sports teams and find that your greatest performers are your worst coaches. I can think of several managers in baseball who were great players but couldn't manage a young team because everything had come to them so easily when they played.

Don't mistake a title—whether it's coach or CEO—for leadership. Positions slot people into an organizational chart; that's all. Real leadership is showing people around you that you're playing to win. Many, many companies fail to recognize the leaders working throughout their organization and, as a result, they will never achieve the levels of success that they should.

One company I consulted with had drastically reduced headcount to save money. They had fired 50,000 people and had 40,000 left. In one meeting, my big question to the executives was, "What are you going to do for the people who are left? You've obviously fired a lot of leadership people and a lot of good folks and the people who are still here are going to have a tough time."

One corporate vice president stood up and said, "If we keep them busy, they won't complain."

I thought it was the saddest comment I'd heard in ages from a corporate executive. My thoughts were that more than half the staff is gone, at least 10,000 of the people left behind are going to miss their friends and former colleagues, and their performance will go down because they won't feel as happy or engaged. Another 10,000 to 20,000 of the remaining staff will wonder if they're going to be next, and their performance will go down because they will try to be invisible. In fact, I was on a flight with a management person from that company, and she described exactly how the recent layoffs were affecting her work.

Let Common Sense Be Your Guide to Leading

I recognized the letterhead she was using, so I asked her if she worked for the company. She said that she was the regional marketing manager.

I asked, "What do you do?"

"Nothing," she said. "Haven't you read the papers? I'm laying low because I don't want them to see me or I may be next."

Now, my first thought was she's supposed to be leading this marketing division, but she's not performing because she's paranoid about losing her job. Her fear filters down to all the people who are working for her, and they stop performing. Her department probably wasn't the only one where things had ground to a halt, so the company was setting itself up for collapse, at least that was my perception.

Instead of doing something to make the transition easier for the people they kept on staff, the company hired an outside firm to create a slogan for the people who were left. They printed it on T-shirts and caps and buttons. The slogan was: I'm a Survivor. I had never heard anything so ridiculous in my life. I went to the corporate president and said, "You know, if you want to win and you want to be a strong company, why would you label 40,000 people as survivors?"

"Well, they still have jobs."

I said, "That's not the important thing. Anybody can have a job. You need to give them some self-worth by telling them they're *winners*. They're the people that you think will take this organization to the next level."

Eventually performance dropped so far that the company was forced to merge with another company. I've never forgotten that example, and it happens in too many companies.

Another company I worked with was struggling with a different kind of transition. They brought in a new person to be CEO and chairman. He was from a very productive corporate environment, one of the top companies in the world, and what happened was very interesting. The company was a service-oriented company, a one-stop shop where you could get almost anything. In their brick-and-mortar stores, you could always find somebody to help you who also had tremendous knowledge of the type of equipment you needed. As a result, the customer service was tremendous.

The first thing the new CEO did was fire those experienced people and hire more part-time and younger workers who knew nothing about the products. Customer service went downhill drastically and the company's main competitor absolutely exploded on the scene. It wasn't until that CEO was removed and replaced that the company was saved. Otherwise they would have gone out of business.

Now the company's doing well again. Why? Because they have a CEO who understands that their leadership is in the individual stores. Their leadership consists of the people who work up and down the aisles. Their leadership, which makes the company much more profitable, is the people who have a range of experience that they bring to the environment, and they let the players play.

The professional baseball team I was with for many years, which was very successful, set a record for the number of consecutive division titles. I worshiped the manager, but I've often said the manager was not the leader. The manager was so important because he let the players lead.

While I was working with that team, a well-known motivational speaker came to a game one day and he asked the manager, "How do you motivate your players?"

The manager said, "I put their names on the lineup card and I let them play."

"There has to be more to it than that."

"No. I just put their names on the lineup card and I let them play."

And he never, in 16 years when I was around him, never made one comment about any player in the press. All of his conversations were private, held with players directly. He put their names on the lineup card and he let them play. We were fortunate enough to have two or three leadership-type people on the team and the manager let them lead. He never called them leaders, and he never gave them a label. He just let them lead, and he let them play.

And I think that's what we're looking for when we talk about leadership. What are the things that really enable you to lead if you decide you want to? Some people may decide they don't want to lead—they may be great followers. I like to think it's about balance. Leaders are not only the people who want to be out front in a visible leadership position all the time. Leaders need to know when to follow; when to let colleagues spread their wings and fly.

I think leadership is an interesting topic because everybody throws the word around. It's a label like "coach." People seem to think that's the hottest and greatest label around these days. But even as everybody tosses these terms around, I don't think they really understand what leadership is.

I gave a lunchtime speech for a major pharmaceutical company. They had a three-hour meeting before the lunch, and invited me to sit in because they were talking about coaching and thought I'd be interested. I took them up on their offer and it really influenced the talk I gave at lunchtime. My first comment when I got up to speak was, "I sat here for three hours in a 'coaching meeting,' and I never heard one thing that dealt with coaching. I heard a lot about training, but not coaching."

Coaching is a very popular term. People like it. People want to be *coached* and they want to be *coaches*, so they use that term, even if what they're really doing is *training*. Training is teaching people basic skills to perform a given task. Coaching is tweaking those skills once a person knows how to play. Coaching is the next level. And it's definitely not the same as leadership.

Unlike coaching, leadership is something that's very fluid. Some people work three, four, or five years before they're respected as leaders. Other people come in and, because of the way they carry themselves, their personality traits, or their ability to communicate, they are seen as leaders from their first day. In many cases that is unfair, but it happens.

Sometimes a label or an old offhand comment about a person overpowers what they actually say and do. For example, one team I worked with had a great young pitcher who was 24 years old. He threw 96 miles an hour. An average fastball is about 89, so he had a lot of talent. But his body language was so negative and aggressive that his teammates didn't like to play behind him in a defensive role. He'd prance around the mound or stare down a guy if he missed a ball. He just wasn't a fun person to be around, so after a period of time we traded him to another team.

That led to an interesting development. The next year we were playing that pitcher's new team in our stadium and I was out by the batting cage. The manager of the other team came over and said, "Dr. Jack, I have a serious question. We've got this pitcher who throws 96, is an amazing talent, but he's driving me nuts. His body language is bad. Players don't like him. He's a disruption in the dressing room, and I don't know what to do about it. I notice that you guys had him last year. What did you do?"

"We traded him to you."

We had a good laugh and that team kept him one more month before trading him to a third team. They kept him one month and then he was released. His career was over at 26 years old because of his body language; not because of his lack of knowledge, not because of his lack of skill, not because of his lack of ability to perform, but his body language.

So it's important to understand the importance of a leader's body language. If you're not the kind of person who likes to pay attention to those kinds of details, then you might not want to be a leader.

Now we're going to look at two different aspects of leadership: assets and liabilities. I think these elements shape everything people do. The assets are the things that make you who you are and make you good at what you do, both personally and professionally. The liabilities are the things that you would like to do better, areas in which you don't feel as competent as you should; in short, those things about yourself that drive you nuts. Everybody has both. I use them with every single person in every single program I do. Whether it's a corporate coaching program, a sales program, or a sport environment, everybody lists their assets and liabilities.

Now, we'll get into detail about those because I think they form the foundation of who we are, what we can or cannot do. In other words, if you have certain expectations of yourself, if others have expectations of you, or if you set short- and long-term goals, your assets and liabilities will determine how you meet them. Before we set expectations and goals, how many of us examine our assets and liabilities? If we don't take into consideration our assets and liabilities, we get ourselves in a bind because we may not be able to do what we set out to. Some people have a liability that hangs over their heads. Those people need to examine that first to figure out how to eliminate it, convert it to an asset, or learn to live with it.

Next, we'll talk about the role of emotion. Emotion makes us who we are. You can look at two people's assets, liabilities, knowledge, and skills and compare them. If they are evenly matched in knowledge and skills, the person who's mentally stronger will win most every time. That's why we put a lot of emphasis on looking at emotional strengths. Let's face it, emotions either become a supplement or a detriment to performance.

It's also important to look at balance. I get so concerned when I go to corporations where people work long hours. Research has indicated that if you're very good at what you do and you work 10 hours a day, 7.5 to 8 of those hours will be productive. It also shows that if you're very good at what you do and you work 13 hours a day, you still get 7.5 to 8 hours of productivity. It's like stretching four years of college into six. Mom and Dad keep paying but you get the same education.

This is why we'll talk about time in terms of quality versus quantity, and that relates directly to balance. I've seen so many people who've worked so many hours that they've destroyed their families. They steal time away from their spouses, children, and friends, they sacrifice their leisure activities, and they begin to hate their jobs because their jobs have stolen everything important to them.

If you're a leader in a corporate environment, you need to help your colleagues understand that work is not who you are, it's what you do. The same goes for leadership. There are a lot of people in positions of power who bring a lot of baggage from the job into their personal lives, which makes them very unpleasant to be around because they get wrapped up in a strange power syndrome. True leaders need to understand that a job is what you do to enable the enjoyment of your personal life.

We'll also talk a lot about commitment in the coming chapters. There are a lot of little, intangible things that separate leaders from other people. We'll examine in detail how personality traits and personality test scores influence leadership. In addition to that, we'll discuss the basic commitment to doing what you do, which I hope will give you some important things to think about.

This book is not an effort to certify you in any way as a leader. It's not an attempt to sway your perception of what leadership is or to give you a rah-rah presentation about what leaders should do and what they are like. It's an attempt to present to you things that will lead you to think about and examine who you are, who you want to be, and where you want to go with your life.

And with that, we will begin to look at some very specific areas within leadership that you might want to think about.

Final Thought

Decide where you are and where you want to be.
Let common sense be your guide.

Chapter 2

Recognizing Your Assets and Liabilities

I t's possible that I have created some confusion regarding the identity and characterization of real leaders, so to gain some clarity, we will talk concretely about what leaders need to do on a daily basis. The following chapters will paint a comprehensive picture of a leader.

Everything leaders are able to accomplish is based on their individual assets and liabilities. Assets are the positive things that make us good at what we do, while liabilities interfere with our achievement. Both can be reflected by specific and measurable factors. It's very important that we're honest when listing assets and liabilities.

What do you think of when you see the terms *assets* and *liabilities*? If you're like most people, you immediately think of accounting and financial statements showing total net worth as measured by money, stocks and bonds, property, and other material things. In this chapter, however, assets and liabilities are defined in less-tangible terms.

Every person, regardless of his or her material assets, has assets and liabilities related to leadership. On the positive side of the ledger are the things we do well, and on the negative side of the ledger are the things we would like to do better or remove from our balance sheet all together to become better overall.

Recognizing these assets and liabilities is particularly important for those with leadership aspirations because leaders are evaluated every day. Colleagues notice how leaders treat other people, what personality that they project, and what body language they have. Many times all these things are results of a person's assets and liabilities, yet in my experience, few people ever take the time to examine these elements deeply or in an organized way.

How often do you observe people avoiding their liabilities, hoping that they won't get in the way? Of course you feel more comfortable with your assets. You like to show them off, and you should. But you also need to recognize your liabilities and share them with other people in order to become better and to stand out from the crowd. Acknowledging your personal strengths and weaknesses makes your talents greater assets to you, your family, your company, and other important areas of your life. In both your personal life and your professional life, it's important that the people on your team can help you to offset or overcome your liabilities.

For example, if you list five assets and five liabilities and you sit down with a group of people you work with in close daily contact, you'll probably find that each of those people has at least one asset to offset one of your liabilities. If you're poorly organized, for example, chances are that a member of your group is super organized. That means that when you're working with the group, you have 10 assets instead of 5 assets and 5 liabilities. If you get into difficulty because of one of your liabilities, you can call on someone who can offset that for you. This is what makes a team. If you're a leader on the team, then you need people to be comfortable making suggestions, especially concerning your liabilities.

A major benefit of recognizing both your positive and negative traits is that it makes you a better person personally and professionally. It also draws you closer to others. Rather than making you reliant on others, it places you in an interdependent relationship in which everyone feels confident. Part of that confidence comes from knowing that you have a good support system. There's always someone who will either supplement your assets or help you offset your liabilities.

It's a puzzle to me when people believe they can develop a plan to win or succeed at their highest level when they do not understand their assets and liabilities. We spend a lot of time developing goals person-ally and professionally. We spend a lot of time talking about winning in some form. We spend a lot of time talking about our beliefs and philosophy, the need to change and do numerous other things. But we spend very little time evaluating our assets and liabilities, even though these are what direct how we fit into the different environments of the world in which we invest our time and energy.

As a leader, recognizing your assets and liabilities—both in yourself and in others—is particularly important because it gives you the foundation you need to surround yourself with the right people. We'll talk about that in Chapter 6, which deals with the team.

Of course, not many people put their liabilities on the table for close scrutiny by colleagues or family members or friends. It takes courage to look at your liabilities when you're alone, but it's even more challeng-ing to expose your areas of weakness to others. However, it is only by recognizing and working with your liabilities that you can remove them, offset them, or neutralize them.

Our corporate culture once was filled with top-heavy companies overloaded with management positions and large workforces. In those cases, there are plenty of people in the environment to blame for failures. Many people never had to recognize or reveal their liabilities and kept them safely tucked out of view. Since then, the corporate landscape has undergone a dramatic upheaval under such names as *rightsizing*, *downsizing*, *reengineering*, or a number of others. Whatever term you use, it means cutting jobs and dismissing people. The resulting smaller organization demands more productivity from fewer people, which consequently means that we need more leaders within the workforce. It means that everyone needs to be transparent about individual assets and liabilities and that in the corporate environ-ment teams need to become much stronger.

After reducing headcount, leaders don't really have the luxury of the blame game. The key to becoming more productive and fostering leadership is to be willing to share with those who have an impact on your life. Begin with the question: Who has an impact on my life? Sit down and take the time to look at your personal team, those closest to you, and your professional team, those in your work environment.

In the corporate environment, it's important that everyone recognize his or her assets and liabilities and those of others on the team. If you're the leader, this is absolutely critical to your growth and your success.

It's not always easy to change a person's assets and liabilities. Your assets are what you have and your liabilities are a part of you as well. Although there are some liabilities you can change or remove, others cannot be fixed and you must not lose sleep over them. Instead, find individuals who can offset the liabilities or people who can help you learn to live with them. This makes for a stronger team, whether it's in your personal or professional life.

If you're a leader, you probably take that role beyond the corporate environment and into leisure time spent with friends. A mutual understanding about your liabilities makes for a stronger team, whether it's your social circle or your professional department. The results will be improved performance and more comfortable relationships for you and your team.

Sharing assets and liabilities will make the team around you feel more important. They will feel they can offer something to your interactions and cooperative work. They will also feel that they can take more risk because someone can offset their liabilities and help them through the process. Productivity will increase naturally as teamwork becomes more efficient and effective.

It does not matter if you're a small team or a large team. Everyone needs a team around them, whether that consists of two people or a hundred people. Every one of those teams, no matter what size, needs a leader. So, if you want to be that person, you need to really make an effort to respect those around you and what they bring to the table.

Let me use a couple of examples here to emphasize the fact that we need to be conscientious about reviewing our assets and liabilities every day. As a leader, you need to evaluate and review not only your own assets every day, but also those of the people around you.

How many of your assets do you take for granted? Think for a moment about the hearing impaired. They are missing one of their senses, but they make optimal use of the ones they have. How many people with normal hearing can read lips? Not very many. Most of us don't have to rely on this skill, so we don't develop it. In fact, deaf people often have an enhanced sense of sight.

It's interesting there has been only one deaf baseball player in history, who played several years in the major leagues. One of those baseball clichés that we hear a lot when talking about defense is that a player "moves at the crack of the bat." Well, this kid couldn't hear the crack of the bat, but his reactions were so incredibly quick because of his visual acuity. That actually made him better than most other out-fielders, and he played several years in the major leagues and was an All-American baseball player in college.

The visually impaired often also develop a stronger sense of hearing. Blind people don't have any special physical abilities that allow them to hear better than sighted people, yet they do. They hear better because they rely so heavily on their auditory assets to learn about their surroundings. You can do a lot more with your assets if you truly want to become better, but you have to decide to be a winner, not a survivor. That's the reason I emphasize that it's important to review your assets and your liabilities every single day.

I played in a celebrity golf tournament one time on Hilton Island. I'll never forget it. One of the celebrities was a blind golfer and he had a foursome with him. It was almost like a movie script. They came up to a water hole, par three, and the four players hit their balls into the water. The blind player was the last to go. His caddy lined him up for the shot, the golfer hit it, and the ball landed within three feet of the cup. He

19

Recognizing Your Assets and Liabilities

walked up and he made the putt. It was interesting because he didn't see the water so it was not a factor for him in the same way it was for his four companions. How many of us see negative things around us and we spend so much time avoiding those things that we forget to look at the positive side?

When I work with athletes, especially golfers, I always tell them, "You know where you *don't* want to go. You don't want to go into the water, but unless you make your last thought about where you *do* want the ball to go, you're going to go in the woods on the left." Never turn away from anything bad unless you're going toward something good. In other words, when you're trying to avoid a liability, make sure that you're trying to use an asset. We spend probably 60 percent of our energy avoiding our liabilities when things are not going well, and we often forget our assets.

I've had corporate people often list their assets and liabilities, and their first comment is, "Jeez, I didn't realize that I had those assets." This happens because they've spent so much time trying to avoid their liabilities that they'd really forgotten how to use their assets to win.

And as a leader, many times you have to be the one responsible for pulling people back emotionally so they don't spend all their time trying to not fail. It is your job to put them on a course where they can succeed, or at least increase the probability that they'll reach their goal.

It's interesting that liabilities present such a different kind of challenge than assets. People either neglect their liabilities or spend so much time trying to avoid them that they do, in fact, lose their assets in the process. It's like a student bringing home two As and one D, then spending all of his time the following semester studying to change the D. As a result, on the next report card the student brings home two Cs and a B.

It's critical that while you're working on your liabilities you develop actions to protect your assets. It's also critical that you put these lists of assets and liabilities in a place where you can see them every morning.

I mentioned that you need to review these lists *every single day*. If you keep them in your mind, like we do so many times with goals, then other things will always come along and let you justify saying that you'll look at them later. By the time you get around to it, you'll be in a mode of avoiding your liabilities because you never set a path to keep you relying on your assets. It's absolutely essential that you write them down and look at them every single day.

It's also critical that you understand that certain things can be on both the assets and the liabilities lists. The biggest category of these things that comes to mind are emotions. If you're an emotional person, that can be a tremendous asset but it can also become a debilitating liability. It's critical that you recognize that it can be on both lists so you can you deal with emotions appropriately.

Another trait that can be both an asset and a liability is aggression. One example of this is that, if you go into a school and ask a teacher about a problem student, many times the first thing they will say is that this student is so aggressive. In class, the student is punished for being aggressive. At three o'clock when the student goes out to the athletic field for after-school practice, he's punished if he's not aggressive.

There has to be some very specific understanding of what the terms on your asset and liability lists really mean. Even on personality inventories you'll see different definitions of aggression. Some people equate it to being assertive while others consider it to be like pushiness or belittling, very negative traits to have. In my opinion it's a positive trait if you make an effort to direct it in a productive way.

I did a study of professional baseball at the minor league level in which we gave personality inventories to 400 hitters, and out of 24 personality traits the only one that differentiated the 0.300-plus hitters from the hitters below 0.300 was aggression. In sport aggression is looked at as a very positive trait. In the corporate environment, many times it's misunderstood, so it's considered to be a negative trait. (We will talk more in Chapter 3 about dealing with personality and performance.)

Now, there are several exercises at the end of this chapter in which you will be asked to list your assets and your liabilities, and then to create a list of measurable actions. These specific, daily actions will help you to either use your assets and evaluate what they have helped you accomplish, or eliminate the impact of your liabilities. As I said before, we all have both, and it's very, very important that everybody in our environment understand the concept of using assets to make us better and helping one another to offset our liabilities.

I think this is of particular importance to leaders because they are the only people in the group who are going to facilitate the recognition of assets and liabilities for every person in the group. I think that it's very difficult to ask other people to do things that you haven't done yourself, so at the very least, leaders need to create those lists for themselves and evaluate them before working with the team to do the same. Having completed the exercise first will give you more confidence to ask other people to do it, and it will also give your team more confidence in you because they recognize that you are willing to share with them.

It's very important to be specific when you are listing your assets and liabilities. When working as a consultant in the corporate environment, I've sent many lists back because they weren't specific enough. One asset that I've heard so often is "I'm a hard worker." That doesn't mean anything to me. Another asset that comes up many times is, "I do the best I can every day." That doesn't mean anything to me either. The idea of doing your best every day is one of my favorite things to talk about. What it really means is that if you have a bad day and you don't do anything, you have a ready-made excuse. You accomplish nothing but you still achieve your goal!

Another popular non-specific asset is, "People tell me I'm a good communicator." Considering the technology and the social media we use every day, there's a terrible misconception that it's an asset to be great in texts and e-mails when, in fact, that has very little to do with communication. If you consider the idea favored in most communication books that 60 percent of communication is nonverbal, as soon as you break out a keyboard you've given up 60 percent of the communication process. It's impossible to be a good communicator without talking. That is a terrible misconception that people have. Being a good communicator means that you're talking with people face to face and you're reading emotions. Being a social media person means that you're very efficient in transmitting information. Assets need to be measurable and specific things that we can evaluate, things that we can put our arms around.

We can get a better idea about the differences between vague and specific assets by looking at a sport analogy. In baseball, a pitcher might say, "I have a good fastball." If that's what it says in the asset column, I send it back to the pitcher and ask what that means. Does it mean the pitch has movement? Is it 90 miles an hour? Whatever the asset, there are so many things that we need to specify, and doing so puts a burden on us because we don't especially like to be measured and evaluated. Despite this, it's crucial to make the effort to make them specific.

The same goes for the liability side. Specificity is key. It's very, very interesting that many times if I have lists of 10 liabilities from a person, I can evaluate that list and most of the time there are no more than three true liabilities; the other seven items are just symptoms of those three. So if I can determine the basic issues on the liability side and we can work toward eliminating one of those issues, six items may come off the list. Now, that's significant because to a person who has listed those liabilities, every single one takes the same amount of emotional energy, whether it's a symptom or an issue. Otherwise, the person wouldn't have listed it. So by eliminating one true liability and basically removing six symptoms, it really gives back a significant amount of mental energy to that person to spend more time pursuing their assets.

Usually, you see this with people in the corporate environment when things are not going well and they quit trying to be winners and start trying to be survivors, which means that they're spending all their time avoiding their liabilities and very little time flaunting their assets. You have to be willing to flaunt your assets. But if you try over a long period of time to eliminate or avoid your liabilities, it's truly possible to forget some of the assets that you have. That's why I've asked you so many times to list them and put them where you can see them every single day.

With many of my athletes, I have them laminate their assets on a business card. Sometimes after a bad at bat, for example, as they go back to the field afterwards, I'll see them peek in their pocket at that card. It takes them about five seconds to realize that they still have their assets. At the last at bat, a player may have looked like he'd never played before, but he still has his assets.

I work with a professional tennis player who keeps his asset and liability list in his bag. If he has a bad set, I see him peek down in his bag and it renews his confidence. It gives him energy and puts him back on the emotional edge where he needs to be. The same is true when you're performing in your job.

I think having this list on hand is probably more important for leaders than others in the corporate environment, especially when things are not going well all the time. My philosophy has always been that if you don't have adversity, then it's really difficult to appreciate success.

We have so many young people coming into the corporate environment today who have never failed, so when they fail in that first job, it's devastating because their toolbox is missing techniques to recover from adversity. They've never spent any time working around their liabilities because parents never let them recognize their liabilities.

I've worked with athletes who are 25 years old but we've had to go back and talk about what went on when they were 12, 13, or 14 because their parents never let them fail or reveal their liabilities. If things weren't going well, the parents would sign them up for another team, so they were always successful. They never learned how to cope with their own weaknesses. I've seen guys' careers end because of that.

When young people come into a corporate environment from college, one of the most difficult things they have to do is learn to recover after experiencing their liabilities, simply because they never had to do that before. A lot of companies hire ex-athletes. Why? Not because they're smarter than other people, not because they're sharper or look the part, but simply because they've learned to experience adversity and recover by focusing on their assets.

I've devoted a whole chapter to talking about recovering from adversity because it's so crucial to the corporate environment and even more so for leaders there. People look to leaders when there's trouble, and they notice how quickly you recover by pursuing a course to flaunt your assets.

I would also ask that you spend serious time making these lists of assets and liabilities, so pick a time when you're not rushed. The most important thing I would tell you is to not prioritize either list. Write down the things as they come to mind so you don't forget anything. There is no hierarchy, so they're all basically on the same level.

After you've done this exercise, you will be prepared for the next couple of chapters, which deal with expectations, goals, and the role of your personality and leadership. Enjoy.

Final Thought

*Build your leadership
style around your assets.*

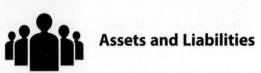

Assets and Liabilities

Personal and Professional Assets

1. _____
2. _____
3. _____
4. _____
5. _____
6. _____
7. _____
8. _____
9. _____
10. _____
11. _____
12. _____
13. _____
14. _____
15. _____

Personal and Professional Liabilities

1. _____
2. _____
3. _____
4. _____
5. _____
6. _____
7. _____
8. _____
9. _____
10. _____
11. _____
12. _____
13. _____
14. _____
15. _____

Recognizing Your Assets and Liabilities

Actions to Show Assets

1. _____

2. _____

3. _____

4. _____

5. _____

6. _____

7. _____

8. _____

9. _____

10. _____

11. _____

12. _____

13. _____

14. _____

15. _____

Actions to Eliminate, Live with, or Transform Liabilities

1. _____
2. _____
3. _____
4. _____
5. _____
6. _____
7. _____
8. _____
9. _____
10. _____
11. _____
12. _____
13. _____
14. _____
15. _____

Chapter 3

Personality and Leadership

E ven though personality is not a topic typically discussed in business books, it's very, very important when we begin to evaluate whether or not a certain person has the leadership traits that we're looking for in a certain position.

Now, it needs to be understood that less is known about leadership, how it's formed, and the role of culture or inheritance than we'd like people to think. We seem to agree that a person's personality, the basic structure, is pretty well established by seven years of age.

One major conflict about personality comes when we try to determine what influences the development of leadership traits. There are two schools of thought. In the first it is believed that 80 percent of personality is inherited and 20 percent is culturally developed. In the other, the inverse is believed: 80 percent of personality is culturally developed and 20 percent is inherited. I would probably lean more toward the first, where 80 percent of personality is inherited and 20 percent is culturally developed. But when we begin to look at basic personality traits, there is confusion about not only how they develop but also in how they are defined.

There are many personality inventories that have been developed over the years to be used to evaluate corporate people, athletes, and others that are going to be involved with a certain group of people. Now, what we need to understand is that many times the results of these inventories are misused because of the different way particular traits are defined by clinicians.

In sport, for example, there is a personality inventory called the Athletic Success Profile that was developed by the Athletic Success Institute. This inventory obviously contains a lot of questions related to sport and commonly used coach and athlete terms. If you want to look at a player's personality, then you would call the Athletic Success Institute and they would administer an inventory and send you a pretty thorough summary of that athlete's traits. The Athletic Success Profile is used by a group called the Major League Scouting Bureau where Major League Baseball teams can join and pay a fee to get the personality summaries for a group of athletes, primarily players they're looking to draft.

The problem with this has been that many teams have been members of the organization for years, but when they get the reports, they put them in a closet and never look at them.

Many years ago when I was the sports psychologist for the Houston Astros, I went into our first meeting and asked if they were members of the Major League Scouting Bureau. They answered that they were, so I asked to review some of the inventories. But the Astros couldn't find them. They turned up in a closet where they had apparently been for years.

The reason I had asked to see them was that I use an inventory developed by psychologist Raymond Cattell, the 16 Personality Factor Questionnaire (16PF). It's a personality inventory developed many years ago and it includes 16 basic personality traits that it scores from 1 to 10. From that 16, the standard scores are weighted to establish eight second-order traits. When I have dealt with corporate groups, the Cattell 16 is the test I've used, and I've also used it with athletes. Since 1975, I've administered as many as 300 to 400 per year for Major League Baseball teams.

The problem with the Athletic Success Profile is that it was developed from the 16PF and they changed a lot of the terminology, so there are many contradictions in the results. If you read about athletes being very coachable on one page, the next page may say that they prefer to make their own decisions and they're not team-oriented, so I never wanted to use that to describe players.

The other thing that needs to be mentioned here is how these scores should be used. There are not only corporate people but also Major League Baseball teams that use these personality scores to rate people and to put them into certain positions on their draft board or organizational chart. I've always been bitterly opposed to that. For example, if you believe a player has major-league talent but his personality profile shows that he may not be the easiest to coach or get along with, and you decide to draft that player, you need to make sure that you have coaches available who can deal with those traits. You also need to have a plan if coaches have issues with that athlete during the season. On teams I've worked with, they could always call me and we could talk about different ways to work through difficulties.

In the corporate environment, personality inventories have been used, and I think misused many times, to hire and fire people. What I've always thought is that—in any environment—talent is an overriding factor. On the one hand, if you have talent and I like that, then it's my responsibility to put you into an environment where your personality serves you best. On the other hand, if you have what I consider a great personality but no talent, there isn't any position I can put you in for success; you're going to fail. So we need to take paper-and-pencil tests and inventories with a grain of salt.

Many researchers over the years have tried to define personality and categorize traits. It's interesting when you look at coaches at the college level. Often they will tell you that they're familiar with the personality traits of their athletes, but many don't realize that what they are seeing are the surface traits, or what we call *external traits*.

Deep-seated personality traits, those referred to as *source traits*, are less evident in performance. It is by observing these surface traits that coaches as well as corporate leaders form a specific idea of the traits that an employee must have in order to succeed. Very few corporate leaders refer to their own personality traits, but they often refer to those of the folks they supervise.

If you put a leader in a corporate environment and allow that person to hire a team, you would find that, in most cases, talent being equal in prospective employees, the leader would hire people with personality traits that are most like his or her own. We found in researching coaches over the years, that they tend to subconsciously recruit athletes who share their personality makeup. If there were conflicts between the coach and the players, it most often involved players who were coached by a previous coach who obviously had different personality traits.

And so it's very important that leaders try to surround themselves with people who have the talent to be very good at their jobs, but that they also make an effort to include different personalities within their team. That's very, very difficult because behavior is the toughest thing to change in an adult. While leaders may be able to make adjustments to the surface traits of their personality, it is unlikely that they will change their core personality traits.

While you could hang your hat on any number of definitions of personality, I like to describe your *source traits* as your *core*, the personality blueprint you were born with. I think over time that your cultural environment does, in fact, cause you to put some of those traits in your pocket and magnify others.

One thing that's very interesting when you look at personality is that what you most often see in people are *surface traits*, what I've always called *sales traits*. These are the traits that people want you to see. I've found that you're more likely to see a person's source personality traits when they're playing golf, and it's sometimes very surprising.

When you administer a personality inventory to someone, they might also be very surprised by some of the traits that you discover.

Over the past 35 years, I have done a lot of research on the personalities of left-handed players versus right-handed players, pitchers versus hitters, new coaches and old coaches, players versus coaches, and in every case I've been surprised at some of the things that I discovered.

The one thing that holds true in almost every environment is that people who are talented and have self-confidence will more often show you their basic personality traits. People, on the other hand, who have self-doubt or a low level of self-confidence many times will try to show you their more appealing surface traits.

As I mentioned earlier, all 16 traits evaluated on the Cattell 16PF is scored 1 to 10. If I'm working in a group, what I like to do is have the people around me score themselves on the 16 traits, and show them the results of the 16PF. Many times the results are pretty consistent with what they expected, but as I said, there are also surprises.

The only reason for this is that people have been taught from a very young age not to show certain traits, aggression being one example. An eight or a nine on aggression might not be accepted in a classroom environment but it is encouraged in a sport environment. Aggression, by one basic definition, is the intent to inflict harm. I don't think that's especially true. I look at a high aggression score as being an indication that a person is stubborn and wants to be the boss, wants to lead the way.

It's not up to me to decide if that is a desirable trait in any corporate environment. It's the leaders' decision whether or not they want people who are high in aggression. Many times if leaders have high aggression scores (e.g., an 8 or a 9), then they don't make very good leaders because they tend to be micromanagers. If I had a choice, I'd rather have someone who was toward the middle on aggression because that person could be a leader when needed and a follower when needed. Someone like that would not stifle the growth and development of team members within the corporate environment.

Now, before we go further, let's take a closer look at the personality makeup as described in the 16PF. Note that each personality trait corresponds to a letter or letter–number combination, but the test does not assign a trait to every letter (e.g., there is no Trait D on the 16PF).

Trait A is *reserved*, meaning introverted, detached, critical, or cool, versus *outgoing*, meaning extroverted, warm-hearted, easygoing, and participatory. There are certain environments where a person needs to be more extroverted than others. Sales positions come to mind. I also think it's very good for a leader in a corporate environment to be middle to higher in extroversion.

Trait B has to do with intelligence. On the lower end of the scale would be someone who thinks more concretely, while the higher end would indicate a greater capacity for abstract thought. This is the most misinterpreted trait on any inventory because a lot of people who are concrete thinkers are very bright people. They figure out ways to get things done using common sense, which I'm all about. More intelligent people who are abstract thinkers don't always have the same common sense.

If as a leader you're looking for someone to work in a computer environment and not interact a lot with colleagues, then you might go more toward an abstract thinker. If you need a get-it-done kind of person who's going to go through trial and error every day until it's right, you may go more toward the middle to the lower end of concrete thinking.

Trait C deals with how a person is affected by feelings. A lower score would indicate that someone is emotionally less stable and more easily upset, whereas a higher score shows that someone is more emotionally stable, meaning he or she faces reality and is calm and mature.

There is something in research called a *critical learning period*, which is the time when things come together for someone in a specific environment. For example, someone in sport may be physically developed and, by all observations, ready to compete, but the package may not have come together as far as emotional maturity, dealing with winning and losing, and other intangible factors. This person hasn't yet gone through a critical learning period and is not really prepared for high-level competition. Despite this, many young people find themselves competing, which is one reason why, I think, 75 percent of kids drop out of sport at 13 years old. They're put into competition before the critical learning period has taken place.

Critical learning periods don't have a set timetable. It's not necessarily going to happen at age 13 or 14. It may be 20 or 25 for some people, so we need to understand when we hire people to look at the talent first. Then, one of your responsibilities as a leader would be to help people who don't appear to be emotionally mature as they deal with adversity and the reality of the corporate environment. It is up to their leader to help them recover more quickly from emotional issues.

Trait E is *humility* versus *assertiveness*. This scores how mild, accommodating, and conforming a person is versus how independent, aggressive, and stubborn. Many traits are defined in different inventories as being aggressive and not aggressive. This particular inventory uses *humble* and *assertive*.

Now, you will find that, depending on the task involved, it may be critical that a person be assertive in order to be successful. In other tasks, it's vital that a person be more accommodating, conforming, and team-oriented to reach a goal. As a leader, you need to understand the role of assertiveness on your team because it's an important factor to have when needed.

Trait F scores how sober a person is, meaning how prudent and serious versus how happy-go-lucky, impulsive, lively, and enthusiastic. There are places for both in the corporate environment. A leader has to know the team and its characteristics, and know what type of person is going to fit in regard to being serious versus enthusiastic and impulsive. I think there are always places for both types of people. I have yet to run across a corporate environment where having fun is a bad thing. There are a lot of people who like to be serious (and I often equate that to the banking industry) but there's no rule that says that you can't have fun and be a good employee. As a leader in the corporate environment, you need to keep that in mind.

Trait G tracks expediency, rule evasion, and a lower sense of obligation against conscientiousness, perseverance, and being bound to rules. I think most of us would agree that, as a leader, you would like to have folks who are on the conscientious side of this trait. It seems that in most every environment in which I've worked, the conscientious person would be much more dependable and much more comfortable to be around.

Trait H is shyness, meaning restraint and timidity, as opposed to social boldness, daring, lack of inhibition, and spontaneity. I've always thought that shy people tend to get mistreated in a corporate environment because they don't "fit the mold." They're not outgoing or up for the spontaneity of a party. This doesn't make them bad people. In most cases they're very good people. They're not venturesome people and maybe that's culturally defined. Maybe they were raised in a nice suburb where kids are supposed to be seen and not heard and go to the right schools and do the right things, and as a result they're basically shy people.

It's interesting that you find more shy people in individual sports even though the pressure is greater than in team sports. I've oriented some athletes away from team sports toward sports like golf and tennis and they have ended up being very good athletes. Their shyness didn't undermine their talent, but it made it difficult for them to feel comfortable and find success in a team environment.

I've always liked to look at Trait I. On one side you have tough-mindedness, self-reliance, and a realistic, no-nonsense approach to life. On the other side you have tender-mindedness, dependence, over-protection, and high sensitivity. This is where sometimes you may see the sales trait, the surface trait, because most people don't want you to think they're tender-minded. Most folks in a corporate environment, as in a sport environment, like to portray themselves as being more tough-minded, more self-reliant. But with more observation, you will eventually be able to see who has a more sensitive source trait.

If you are a leader in a corporate environment, you probably want people who are in the middle of the scale. You want people to be independent, but you also want them to be willing to be dependent in certain situations. In other words, you want them to be willing to ask for help from their colleagues or from the leader, so being in the middle is probably good.

If you're looking at a sport environment, you probably want people to be more toward the tough-minded side. This means they come to work every day, they are work-oriented and self-reliant; and if they know how to play the game, they play it hard and they play it well.

Trait L concerns being trusting versus suspicious. I think the interpretation of this trait has changed over the years. Years ago trusting people would be seen as being free of jealousies, easy to get along with, and pretty adaptable, and I think a lot of people still score highly on that trait. But the suspicious side of the trait, where people are self-opinionated and hard to fool, I think you're seeing more in young people. They're not afraid to ask leaders for reasons *why* they should do something. As a leader, when you ask somebody to do something in a corporate environment and they ask why, the wrong answer is: *Because I'm the leader.* The right answer is whatever reason that you're asking them to do a certain task. People deserve to know why they're being asked to do things, and in today's environment they seem to be much more willing to ask those questions.

Now, Trait M is *practicality*, being careful, conventional, and proper versus *imaginative*, which is being careless of practical matters. I've always thought that it's kind of exciting to have people who are both sides of this trait. Being practical is very good and it works in many cases, but imaginative people have creative skills that are also very appropriate in many corporate environments. So as a leader, you need to be appreciative of both.

Trait N is *forthrightness*, being natural and sentimental, versus *shrewdness*, which is being calculating and penetrating. I've always enjoyed dealing with forthright people. I think that many times if people are on the shrewd side of this trait they carry an air of secrecy that is not very helpful in a corporate environment.

Q1 is *conservative*, respecting established ideas, versus *experimenting*, which is critical, liberal, analytical, and free thinking. Like the practical–imaginative trait, I think it is very healthy to have experimenters on a corporate team in addition to having just enough conservative people to keep the balance right.

Q2 is *group dependent*, which includes people we might describe joiners or real sound followers, as opposed to *self-sufficient*, which means people who prefer their own decisions and being resourceful. Obviously it's good to be resourceful and to have confidence in the decisions you make, but at the same time, you need to be able to appreciate the greater good of the team as opposed to whatever personal advantage you might get by making a certain decision. So again, as a leader, this is one of those traits that are kind of interesting for keeping you on your toes, and you probably need a bit of both.

Q3 tracks a person's discipline and their threshold for self-conflict. I love this trait. On one end, you have people who are careless of protocol and follow their urges; on the other side you have people who are controlled, socially precise, and act in a way that upholds their self-image. Now, it depends on what your self-image might be, but I find in most definitions of personality that the other side of undisciplined self-conflict is strong self-discipline. It's very important in most corporate environments that you have some level of self-discipline. It doesn't have to be incredibly high. It needs to be high enough so you accept accountability and you make changes when necessary. So again, it's one of those traits that it might be interesting to have people from both sides of the scale on the same team.

Q4 is the person's level of relaxation, which is the state of being tranquil and not frustrated as opposed to tense, which means that you're frustrated and driven and overwrought many times. In sport, it's nice to have players who are in the middle on that trait. If you buy the idea that you're going to be the best performer if you approach every task at as high an emotional level as you can control, then if you're on the low side of the relaxation spectrum and you get very frustrated in performing a task, then at worst your attention or anxiety level may increase, but only to the middle range, which means you're still basically under control. However, if your source trait for levels of relaxation and attention are typically about 7 on the 10-point scale, and you get frustrated, then your anxiety level spikes to somewhere between 8 and 10, which means you're out of control. That's why it's nice to be at the middle or low end on that particular trait.

Now, what we try to do is take those 16 traits and come up with a standard score in what are called second-order traits, and those traits include leadership, independence, and anxiety level. Those are the kind of traits that we look at many times in a corporate environment—and in 40 years of using this test, I've never attempted to tell a corporate person that they should be a leader because they're high in the leadership trait on this inventory. As we said before, there are different types of leadership, that which is inherent and that which is assigned. There are any other number of ways that you can categorize leadership, but I've always thought that it's earned through performance. And when I say *earned*, I mean that you gain your teammates' respect through your performance. After you've gained that respect, then your personality plays a role in your leadership going forward.

The best leaders that I've ever been around were people who either didn't want to be leaders but were great performers, or those who performed well and let their leadership be determined by the way they played the game.

I think the same thing holds true in a corporate environment. Leadership is earned and once that respect is lost, it's virtually impossible to get it back unless you change environments because a level of suspicion develops in the work force. Your colleagues begin to wonder why you're making certain decisions or trying to get close to them when you just did something to lose their respect. And so it's virtually impossible to get leadership back once you've lost it.

Suffice it to say that personality plays a very important, even critical, role in leadership, but it needs to be approached in a very common-sense manner. I find it difficult to understand why people are evaluated more on personality than performance. That happens a lot in corporate environments and I don't think there's an excuse for it. I think if you hire people to do a job, then their performance should be based on whether or not they do the job.

You've got to realize when you hire people that they are who they are. You can't expect them to change. As I said before, the toughest change to make is a behavioral change. It takes a very long time even if change is successful. And most of the time, if a behavioral change is made, it's made in the surface traits. It doesn't flow down to the source traits. Once your blueprint for personality is developed, it's there. From that point on, you make decisions when you're growing up about whether or not to reveal particular traits to people. And some traits you keep in your pocket your whole life. You may be an eight on a certain trait, but you never show it because it's not appropriate in the environment in which you work.

As a leader in a corporate environment, when you have several people who look to you for leadership, you need to understand that everybody's different. When you try to assemble a group of people with the same personalities, it's not going to work most of the time. You need variety. You need people who are sometimes going to challenge you.

And the only way you become a better leader is to understand that it's supposed to be challenging. How would you ever appreciate a good environment if you never had challenges and adversity? Look at personality as an important factor, as good knowledge to have, but don't look at personality as determining whether or not you're going to hire somebody. It just doesn't have a good end result.

Final Thought

Be who you are every day.
Let your team see your personality.

 **Personality**

Personality Traits Needed for Leadership

1. _____
2. _____
3. _____
4. _____
5. _____
6. _____
7. _____
8. _____
9. _____
10. _____
11. _____
12. _____
13. _____
14. _____
15. _____

Actions to Show Your Personality to Your Team

1. _____
2. _____
3. _____
4. _____
5. _____
6. _____
7. _____
8. _____
9. _____
10. _____
11. _____
12. _____
13. _____
14. _____
15. _____

Chapter 4

Goals and Leadership

I n Chapter 2 you examined your assets and liabilities and recognized the fact that you need people around you to offset your liabilities. In Chapter 3 you examined your personality traits and determined which ones are necessary to be in a leadership role. The next step is to establish goals.

It's always been a bit confusing to me when companies write five-year goals and then they revise them every year for the next five years. It's always made much more sense to me to set goals for no more than a year at a time and to be able to reflect on them so that everything you do every day relates to your 12-month outcome. This avoids the possibility of wasting energy by getting off track and having to recover. But, more important, by setting goals every day, I think you become much more focused, you know what you need to do and when you need to do it. To do this, you need to make sure that your goals are such that you can examine them every single day and determine whether or not you at least made progress.

To do this there are basically four characteristics goals need to have. The first is that they need to be specific. Doing the best you can is not a goal. Working hard is not a goal. Even working 12 hours is not a goal. Goals are specific when they give you direction.

When I work with corporate individuals and I see overly general goals, then we go back and reexamine them, break them down, and analyze them so we may try to come up with very specific things that we can measure at the end of the day.

47

The second trait of successful goals is that they need to be difficult every day. If a goal is not difficult every day, then you find that you get into a mode of complacency and you don't really make yourself better every day. And if you don't improve and learn something new, then I'm not sure why you would set goals in the first place.

If all you want to do is survive, then goal setting is obviously not a necessity. But if you want to win and you want help your team win and you want to set an example for your team as a leader, then you make your goals difficult so that people around you know that you're trying to get better every day.

The third key in setting goals is that they need to be time oriented. In other words, you need to set goals and put a time limit on them so that you can evaluate and adjust if you need to.

The fourth thing, which I think is the most important, is that goals need to be attainable. It's psychologically devastating to set a goal for the day and at two o'clock in the afternoon to realize you're not going to get there. To keep your sanity, you lower your goal so that you can feel some type of achievement. It's not healthy. It's much better to set goals for every two hours or three hours so that when you achieve that, you can raise the bar. Psychologically it's better for you, it makes you feel better about who you are, it makes you feel better about what you're trying to do, and it also keeps you on track. So being attainable is critical, but at the same time you need to strike a balance between trying to push yourself and making them overly difficult.

Now, after you've set goals, it's a really good idea to go back and review Chapters 2 and 3, which deal with assets and liabilities and personality. It's easy to set goals and then try to get there without examining your assets and liabilities. It makes no sense to set goals that you cannot achieve because you don't have the assets you need. It doesn't make you a bad person. It doesn't make you an unintelligent person. It's just a reality check that everybody needs to go through every day: These are my goals and I have the assets to achieve them. That's a major boost.

As I previously mentioned, when I deal with athletes, we laminate their goals on a business card so that they have their goals where they can see them all day, every day. It takes five to ten seconds to review that list, and it keeps you on track, not only with understanding where you are professionally, but also understanding whether you can achieve what you set out to achieve that day.

It's a boost to your system. It gets you back to what we like to call the *emotional edge*. It gets you back to a point where your emotions become assets in your work as opposed to being detriments. It's critical that you keep your assets list close by when you're examining your goals. And it's also good to know that if you set goals and you don't have the assets to get there, you can look at your liability list and determine who on your team can offset those liabilities and help you achieve your goals. This is where we begin to see better teamwork—when you involve other people. And as a leader, it's critical that you do this. You begin to involve other people with the achievement not only of your goals but also of the team goals. This also makes it necessary to examine the team goals so that your own are consistent with them.

This sounds simple. As a leader, aligning individual and team goals should be a part of your commonsense leadership, but most of the time it's not. Instead, we get complacent in our environment, we get lose sight of our goals, and then it takes a lot of energy to get back on track. We probably waste about 60 percent of our energy thinking and worrying about things we can't control. If you could get back 50 percent of that wasted energy and apply it to achievement, then you're going to be much more effective, not only as a teammate but also as a leader because people see how you use your energy. And I keep repeating the old cliché: What you are talks so loudly people can't hear what you say.

That's basically how leadership is determined, by people observing you as the leader, your work ethic, and your ability to stick with your goals and stay on track.

You also need to relate your goals back to your personality. Many times I find that in dealing with corporate individuals they have personality traits that prohibit them from achieving certain goals. That doesn't make you a bad person. It's just a fact that certain personality traits are necessary to achieve certain goals. And if you in particular don't have the necessary traits, then you need to involve teammates who do. Involving people in goal achievement is a team asset.

Over the years, I've worked with so many athletes who set 12-month goals and then don't look at them again until well into the season—and sometimes not until almost a year later. Probably the best example was a player I met during baseball spring training. He told me, "I'm going to quit and I want to take you to dinner." And so we went to dinner. It was March 12th, just before the start of the season. I asked him, "What do you hope to achieve by the end of October?" He gave me very specific numbers, including such things as batting average, RBIs (runs batted in), base hits, on and on.

I said, "Well, if you're going to quit anyway, let's play a game. Humor me for a while." I took a stack of napkins and I said, "Okay, if this is what you want to achieve specifically by the end of October, what do you want to achieve by July, the All-Star break, which is the middle of the season, in regard to this goal?" He wrote it down.

And then I said, "What do you want to achieve by Opening Day, April 1st, that relates to your goal?" And he wrote it down. And then I asked him, "What do you want to achieve tomorrow, March 13th, that relates to your goal?" And he wrote it down.

And I said, "Okay, what do you want to achieve in each at-bat tomorrow and what do you want to achieve in each swing tomorrow?" He wrote all that down and we did that for every specific category that he had included in his 12-month goals. We used a stack of napkins.

Well, to make a long story short, he didn't quit. Every week we would go over those numbers and by the end of the season he had significantly surpassed every single number that he had set on his achievement list. It wasn't magic; it was common sense. If you make everything you do every day important to your eventual outcome, then you avoid wasting energy by going off track and having to recover. You basically begin to use most, if not all, of your energy every day to achieve something specific.

I did that same exercise with a corporate individual recently. We sat down and we talked about what he wanted to achieve at the end of the year in productivity. We worked backwards, starting with the 12-month mark, which he thought was quite odd. But six months into the program, he was far beyond everything that he had hoped to achieve by that benchmark.

What this means basically is that the process is critical. If you don't execute the steps well on the way to 12 months, you can't get that lost time back and there's no way to make up for it as your deadline approaches. So every single day you must execute whatever process is necessary to achieve something during that specific day.

I spend a lot of time with everyone who I work with talking about the process. For example, in baseball if you execute the process well—you have good swings and you hit the ball hard—and you go 0–4, to me it was not an 0–4 day because the process was good in every single at-bat. To me, you had a 4–4 day, you just didn't get any base hits. But if you keep hitting the ball hard and you keep swinging the bat well, those hits will come. You can't hang your hat on end results, but if you've executed the process well, you can hang your hat on the process.

Many times, especially in the corporate environment, you find that people set goals for you. I have strong reservations about that because I think that the people who set them don't really understand an individual's assets and liabilities or what a team is capable of, and all that

51

Goals and Leadership

factors into the end result. Too often, the people who set goals are more involved with revenue and stockholder value, and they lose track of what the assets and liabilities are: the workforce.

Many years ago I worked with a company that was one of the largest hazardous waste disposal plants in the United States. They called me in to work with middle management, and from there we worked up and down. When I went into the plant, they were disposing of 3 million pounds of hazardous waste a month. Then, I went up to the corporate office, which was up on the hill in a really nice building, and I talked to the executives about what they wanted to achieve.

The response was, "Well, we need to do more than 3 million pounds a month."

I said, "Well, what are you doing to help your workforce understand where you're trying to go?"

The answer was, "We told the workforce we need to increase to 4 million pounds a month."

And I said, "Well, what did you do in addition to that?"

"That's all we did. If they do what they're supposed to do, they'll achieve it." They mentioned that they had considered keeping the plant open longer hours, including on weekends, but the workers had refused to come in.

I went back to the plant and was very interested to learn that they had all heard the goals from the corporate office but they had not been educated on the process to make the increase in productivity happen. At this point in the day I needed to use the bathroom, so I asked where it was. The workers told me there was no bathroom. This company had just completed a $10 million renovation in the plant and there were no bathrooms. Instead, they had porta potties.

I went back up to the corporate office and I asked, "Why didn't you put bathrooms in?"

Their response was, "It wasn't in the architectural plan. We just forgot to do it."

"Where do your workers change clothes?"

"They change in the car or before they come to work."

"Where do they take a break?"

"They walk outside."

Things were becoming much more clear to me. When I went back down to the plant, I looked around and I put myself in that environment and I tried to determine what we needed to do. I came up with the idea to institute a program where the plant's processes were evaluated. I also found out by asking questions what the workers liked to do in their off time.

Armed with this knowledge, I went back to the executive office. I said, "These workers like to hunt and fish on the weekends. They're not opposed to working on weekends, but they think they've done all they can during the week. They would also like to have a place to take a break. They would like to have somewhere to walk around other than just walking outside of the plant."

Now, it's very important here to note that if you have workers who are disgruntled, you have low morale, and the last thing you want to do is to provide a gathering place so they can talk each other into being negative. The corporate office took this into consideration and made a few key changes. They put a track around the plant so the workers could walk during their breaks. They also put mobile homes inside the plant area so they had a place to take a break that was still nearby. The mobile homes also had showers so workers could change clothes and clean up before they went home, and they didn't have to use their cars anymore. They also put a horseshoe pit and basketball court out behind the mobile homes. Finally, the organization went out then and leased 1,500 acres close to the plant (at a very affordable price) so that the workers would have a place to hunt and fish. It was very interesting that, in addition to the reeducation process about how to reach the increased goals, we had changed the basic environment and given them the perception that the company cared about them. (We will talk more about the environment in Chapter 7.)

Over time, within the next two to three months, they had increased production to 5 million pounds a month. They were happier people. They knew they had a place to go on the weekends. They knew when they took a break they had a diversion from the plant. And it was, to me, a very simple, commonsense solution to what had become a morale problem in the plant.

Everyone was satisfied with the progress, then in one meeting the director of human resources said, "I've got an idea. If one of the departments sets a record, we'll go visit them, shut the plant down, call that department up, congratulate them, and give them pen and pencil sets with the company logo on top." I thought that was the strangest thing I'd ever heard. If you're going to give them something, give them a gift certificate so they can take their families to dinner.

But they decided to go ahead with the human resources plan. It didn't go over very well. The first month they called a group together and congratulated them, they gave them a pen and pencil set. The next day, of the 40 pen and pencil sets they gave out, 35 were back on the human resources director's desk because the workers had no use for them.

So we made a revision to the plan and gave them a certificate to go to dinner instead, and that went over very well. People were excited about it. It's a reward. It's not the size of the reward or the cost of the reward. It's the fact that they're being recognized for achieving specific goals. And it's very important that you, as a leader, make sure that your team is recognized for things that they accomplish.

Too often we're limited in our positive reinforcement and liberal in our negative reinforcement. However, we know from research over many years that negative reinforcement may be effective for the short term, but positive reinforcement is going to cause long-lasting results.

You know, there's nothing more critical than employee buy-in to goals. That example at the hazardous-waste plant illustrates that employees need to be able to feel and taste the goals. They need to be able to get a real piece of the success that comes with goal achievement. There are many times when the goals are proven to be unattainable or unacceptable. If that's the case, leaders don't wait until they get deep into the process before they begin to recognize that these goals are inappropriate. Maybe they're not achievable because of a lack of equipment or a workforce shortage. Any number of things may prohibit you. It doesn't mean you're incapable of getting there, but there may be peripheral things that are inhibiting the achievement of goals.

As a leader, it's your responsibility to notice the soft spots around the workforce; to notice that your people are working hard, they're bright people, and they're doing whatever they can to make things happen, but as a team you lack certain things that are necessary to enable you to achieve. You, as a leader in the group, are in a position to make changes and analyze what's happening on a daily basis. And you really shortchange your team if you don't address these issues with the appropriate people who can make changes. What that means is that you need to be a leader; you need to perform and let your teammates see you do it, but you also need to be a coach. You need to coach your people, but it's just as important that you're able to *coach up* as you communicate with the people above you.

I had an experience with a company whose CEO was a marketing person, but operations wasn't doing well. He hired an operations manager with a good reputation, who changed the procedures and the mechanics of how the company was working. As a result, the company began almost immediately to perform much better. Six months into this change, the CEO fired the operations manager.

I asked him, just out of curiosity, "Why did you fire him?"

Goals and Leadership

He said, "In six months, he never taught me anything about operations."

Now, many people would think that's unfair, but to me it made sense because it's very important that leaders are able to not only lead their team but also, in some instances, to become a coach to people above them. That makes them feel better about giving you what you need to get the job done.

Leadership isn't only about protecting your team and being a leader to them; it's about including upper management in the process. Even though upper management many times is not involved with day-to-day operations, they appreciate when the leader on the team lets them know what's going on, what needs to happen, and what they need to become better. As a leader of the team, when you're dealing with your goals, it's important that you make sure that upper management understands what it takes to execute those goals.

One particular company I worked with in hazardous-waste disposal passed down the word through five or six levels of management about a cost-savings plan. If you have any common sense, you know that the orders and the directions change with every level of management that they pass through. It's almost like a game of telephone that you might have played when you were a kid. One person whispers a story to somebody else and it goes all the way around the room and, by the time it comes back to you, it's a completely different story because everybody puts their own interpretation on it. Two things are important here. First, directions need to be very specific and there should be nothing left to interpret.

In this particular company, they were cutting back. On the plant floor, they put hazardous waste in big barrels, and there's a yellow line that the barrels must not cross. There also are a bunch of other regulations. One day inspectors from the federal Occupational Safety and Health Administration (OSHA) came in and they found a violation.

The top of one barrel wasn't secured and OSHA fined the company $100,000.

What had happened was that a worker was locking the lid on a barrel and noticed that another barrel was over the yellow line a little bit. In his pursuit of saving time and money, he stopped what he was doing and went over to push that barrel back into place—then he forgot to go back and finish his original task. He left the barrel unlocked. In a room of about a thousand barrels, OSHA came in and found that one unlocked barrel and fined the company $100,000.

Now, if the company had really communicated specifically how to get where they wanted to go in cost savings, the worker would have been able to shut the first barrel and then go move the other barrel back over the yellow line. Instead, he chose to do things as quickly as possible and it cost the company a lot of money.

So many times workers are confused because they hear the goals but they don't hear any explanation of how to get there. Many times the goals are sent down through the system without any attention to the workforce's assets, liabilities, and personality; and, in turn, people are put in a very uncomfortable position because they're doing what they can and it doesn't match up with the goals they were given.

It's critical that everyone up and down in a company understands what needs to be done in a very specific way, as I said before, so that nothing is left to perception.

In the next few pages, you're going to be asked to list your goals and action plans to get there. You'll also learn firsthand how to examine your goals by working backwards, and then how to communicate those goals to the people who are responsible for getting there. You continue to evaluate and to adjust and to be flexible as you go through this process because, as we will learn in Chapter 5, people don't leave jobs many times because of money. They don't leave because of a position. They don't leave because of the work environment. They leave because they've never been given specific instructions other than to work hard and do their jobs.

Have fun with your goals, and in the next chapter we're going to talk about expectations and how important it is to evaluate your assets, liabilities, personality, and goals when you're writing your self-examinations. Too many times these things are looked at separately. These first five chapters are critical in setting a foundation for who you want to be and where you want to go.

Final Thought

Evaluate Your Goals Every Day

 **Goals**

Goals as a Leader

For every long-term goal, list related short-term goals. Each statement must be specific, and each goal must be difficult but attainable within the stated time frame.

Goal A:

 A-1: _____

 A-2: _____

 A-3: _____

Goal B:

 B-1: _____

 B-2: _____

 B-3: _____

Goal C:

 C-1: _____

 C-2: _____

 C-3: _____

Goal D:

 D-1: _____

 D-2: _____

 D-3: _____

Goal E:

 E-1: _____

 E-2: _____

 E-3: _____

Personal Goals

Goal A:

    A-1: _____

    A-2: _____

    A-3: _____

Goal B:

    B-1: _____

    B-2: _____

    B-3: _____

Goal C:

    C-1: _____

    C-2: _____

    C-3: _____

Goal D:

    D-1: _____

    D-2: _____

    D-3: _____

Goal E:

    E-1: _____

    E-2: _____

    E-3: _____

Chapter 5

Expectations and Leadership

Very simply put, you need to expect to win every day. It's critical to define winning as not only doing well professionally but also touching people's lives. Expecting to win at least puts the probability of doing so on your side. There are no guarantees, but if you don't expect to win, you have negative expectations, making the probability that you will do well virtually zero.

Before we really discuss the topic of expectations, I think it's important to define *winning*. Too often we attach the concept of winning only to those people who lead the team in sales, those people who at the end of the year are given awards for being the best. In sport we talk about winning as the team that has more runs, more touchdowns, or more points.

In the context of expectations, I would like you to define winning as *executing the process well*. As we discussed in the last chapter on goal setting, all you can do is ensure that you perform well; winning is basically out of your control.

Recently I worked with a pitcher who was bothered by his record, even though at the end of the year he had the best numbers of his career. His record was 0.500, but in his mind, he did not pitch very well. We sat and talked about the fact that once you throw a pitch, you don't control what happens afterward. You don't control the outcome, but you can control how well you execute. The rest usually takes care of itself.

The same principle holds true in business. If you're a leader on your team, all you can do is execute correctly every day, have a strong work ethic, flaunt your assets, try to eliminate your liabilities, have realistic goals—and expect to do well as a result.

I would like one expectation of everybody, whether in sport or business, to be to have fun. Have fun at what you do. Not the laughing, screaming, hugging kind of fun, but rather personal fulfillment that you did something well that day.

One thing you can do to almost ensure that positive things happen is to have one of your expectations be to touch somebody's life every day. Success is not about money. It's not about achievement. It's about helping other people. If you set out every single day to touch some-one's life and you, in fact, do that, it goes a long way in solidifying your reputation as a leader. Touching someone's life may be as simple as a friendly hello or a pat on the back. It doesn't have to be some magnificent, striking thing that you do. It's just a way to show other people that you care about them.

One of the biggest struggles that I've had to deal with in my career is trying to get clients to expect to do well every day. We basically grow up being taught to respond to negative expectations. If you have children, the question I ask is, "When was the first time you ever said *no* to an infant?" It probably was when they were two or three days old. It's not a malicious no but it could be in response to trivial things such as lying on their stomach or knocking the mobile off the bed. Once babies get to crawling, they hear, "No, don't crawl here; don't crawl there." Parents put up the gates. By the time they get into tee-ball, they hear so many negative comments from coaches and parents.

I wrote a book called *Let Them Play*, which was to help parents and coaches make the environment better for kids. Through research, I'd determined that 75 percent of kids drop out of sport at 13 years old. It has always bothered me that so many kids drop out of an activity that probably teaches more life skills than any other kids can go through— and there has to be a reason. One reason could be they've been in competition eight years, and maybe they've had enough. But another likely reason is the number of times that they've had negative feedback from coaches and parents over those eight years.

Years ago I had two sons in tee-ball; one was four and the other, five. One day I went to the park, which was a pretty bad park. Two weeks earlier a parent had shot at an umpire. And so with that in mind, I sat and watched a game.

I'll never forget what I saw. There was a four-year-old who was swinging the bat. In tee-ball, there is no pitcher. Instead, the ball is on a tee at just the right height for kids, and they swing until they hit it. Well this boy kept missing, but he got tired of swinging, so he went and sat down and started crying. Instead of consoling him, the coach went over and picked him up by his shoulders and literally threw him over the fence. The kid hit the ground on his knees and started running toward the woods, and the coach yelled after him, "Don't ever come back to this park with that whiny attitude."

I start looking around for the kid's parent because I think we're going to have some action. But the guy next to me nudged me and said, "Dr. Jack, the coach is his dad." What a fun family it must be! I wonder how many times kids in that family are told no.

The next season I signed up to coach, and I wanted to provide a good environment. I wanted kids to expect to come and play and have fun every single day and walk away with smiles on their faces. On my team I had 14 kids who had obviously never seen a baseball. At that time I worked with the Braves, which really impressed the parents, so they kept telling their kids that we were going to win it all. Well, the kids didn't have a clue who the Braves were.

On the first day of practice, parents brought their kids to the field 30 minutes early so they could claim the best positions. The parents would run up to me asking, "How are you going to pick positions? My son wants to play left field! My son wants to play shortstop!" I just kept thinking that these kids are four and five years old. So I asked everyone to sit down so I could show them how we were going to pick positions.

I told the kids to run out on the field and sit down somewhere. And they did. I looked at the parents and said, "That's where they play." We changed positions every game and we had fun.

I'll never forget the first game. My son, who was five, had come with me to the Braves' stadium a lot and, of course, picked up some habits. He comes up to bat the first time and takes off his warm-up jacket. It's about 90 degrees. Then, he starts adjusting his batting gloves. And, of course, the ball is sitting on a stick right in front of him. Finally, he steps in and he's got a big wad of bubble gum in his jaw, and he's spitting and digging. I'm just hoping he hits it. He does and the ball goes about 10 feet. I was at third base and I started hollering to him, "Run, Hunter, run." Well, he ran straight to me instead of to first. And he didn't just run—he slid. He got up and was wiping the mud off his shirt. I didn't want to embarrass him because I wanted him to be having fun. So I put my arm around him and said, "Son, I don't know who made the rules out here—it wasn't me—but they're telling me that when you hit the ball, you're supposed to touch that base over there first. That's probably the reason they call it *first*."

And he said, "Okay, Dad." Then, he slid into home. I don't know what he heard, but that's what he did. So I ran down to home plate and got over the umpire and started yelling, "He's safe, isn't he?"

The umpire looked up with this pitiful look and said, "Yes, sir, I guess he is safe."

The parents on the other team are hollering, "He ran the wrong way! He ran the wrong way!"

And I went over and leaned up against the fence, and I said, "Folks, we're going to worry about direction next year. This year we're just going to hit it and run."

It was a fun beginning to the year. And parents understood where I came from in regard to enjoying the game and having fun. I didn't care what they did because I wanted them to have a good time. I wanted to see all my kids playing again next year.

After that game, I went over to the field where my other son, Tripp, was playing. I didn't see him on the field, so I asked the coach, "Coach, where's Tripp?"

"Left field," he said.

And I said, "Coach, you need to look again."

Tripp had used a rock to prop his glove up facing home plate so it would be caught if somebody hit a fly ball out there. Then, he'd gone to play on the swings with his sisters. I love it when a plan comes together, so I just waited in the car for him after the game. Of course, he had to go back and get his glove.

When he got to the car and he said, "Dad, we won again."

And I said, "Son, you are a special athlete."

I always look back on that as one of the most fun experiences I've ever had and I hope the kids on my team feel the same way. From that first team I coached, there are kids who still call me to talk. And that's important to me.

I always ask corporate groups, "How many of you expect to have fun every single day?" Most of the time about 10 percent raise their hands and that bothers me because not enough of us enjoy what we do. We work, we make money, we pay the bills, we raise a family, but we don't really get fulfillment from our jobs.

I think it's the job of a leader to make sure that the people on their team have fun, get fulfillment, and enjoy what they do. I know for a fact that some days are much worse than other days. But I also know that if you work hard enough, at the end of the day you can find something that was good. So you need to understand that expectations are very important.

Now, here's the most important thing to remember about expectations: When you set your expectations, you need to go back and review the last three chapters on assets and liabilities, personality, and goal setting. Because if your expectations don't match up with those three things, then it's very hard to have fun at what you do. So there has to be some coordination of what you bring to the party and what you need to do within the job to flaunt your assets and make sure that you can achieve your goals.

As I mentioned before, it's a fact that most people leave their jobs not because of money or position or title. They leave their jobs because they don't know what's expected. It's critical that your expectations for each role be very specific and clearly communicated.

What we're going to look at in the rest of this chapter is how expectations are formed. Too many times I find that my clients are performing to others' expectations as opposed to their own. When I sit down with clients, the first thing I have them do is list their personal and professional expectations. I'd like you to do the same when you get to the exercises at the end of this chapter. Be very specific. Next, write down what you think other people expect of you, personally and professionally. Then write down what you think is expected of you by your teammates, the folks who work with you in your immediate area of the company.

What happens is, because all of us want to belong to something, we tend to gear ourselves toward the expectations of other people. When you work to please other people, you begin to lose track of your personal expectations because you lose track of your assets and spend more of your time trying to avoid your liabilities. And so it's very important that you understand the expectations of other people and how they fit with the ones you have for yourself.

As a leader, it's critical that you sit down with your team and have them list what they think you expect of them and what they expect of themselves. Then, look at your own list of what you expect of them. You're going to find some interesting results.

Number one: You're going to find that many times people's expectations are not similar to those that you have of them. It's hard to have a cohesive team unless everybody knows everybody else's expectations. Once you get that settled, then it becomes a pretty workable team. At least it becomes a workable team in that the probability of succeeding is shifted to your side.

Because of the social and economic environment, there are so many people who spend most of their time trying to please the people around them because they worry about losing their jobs. One of the most important things we can do—and we can do it through expectations—is to help people understand how important they are to the team success when it comes to winning, not simply survival.

If we get back to the point that I was making about kids and the word *no*, it's interesting to note that by the time kids are 18 and finish high school, in a normal home they've been told what not to do an average of about 200,000 times. For example, if they get 80 percent on an exam in school, they're criticized for the 20 percent they missed. They don't get the positive reinforcement that was common in past years in education.

I think teachers are now more focused on test scores than learning, and that's created a very difficult environment for kids in regard to expectations about learning life skills, how to recover from adversity, how to deal with other people, how to lead, and how to feel. There's a list that's a mile long of things that kids could learn in school if there were more positive reinforcement and the expectations were conveyed by teachers that success was expected in regard to learning, not necessarily just in regard to test scores.

I have so many pitchers in baseball over the years who have spent so much time trying *not* to throw bad pitches, trying to *not* give up hits, trying to *not* do things, that they almost forget their assets and instead spend their time trying to not fail. And I understand why. When you get into the world, we almost have to experience a major attitudinal upheaval as far as expecting to do well because adulthood is not what we lived with for the first 18 to 21 years. Once you get your team to the point that they do, in fact, expect to do well, then life becomes more fun for everybody.

I've been in sports psychology for 45 years and I can honestly say I've never had a bad day at work. I've had challenging days, obviously, which have made me better. I've tried to learn something new every day. But when I look back at every single day, something good happened. For example, if one of my pitchers pitched a good game but the team lost, to me was not a bad thing. So many times we gloss over the little things that mean a lot in regard to the big picture, and we really lose track of this whole expectation process. To keep the right mindset, you need to do several things: First, you need to make sure that there's some consistency between your goals, your expectations, the probability that you're going to do well, and the possibility that you can do well. Once you've done that and put the package together, you will find that leadership is easier because everybody understands each other better.

I remember years ago when I was with one baseball team, our third baseman was the leader on the team. Every day, he got up and he expected good things to happen. He never talked about it to teammates really, and he never, you know, flaunted his assets around, but his work ethic was incredible, his dedication was amazing, his ability to have fun every day was remarkable, and the teammates around him picked up on his attitude, and he became the leader, even though he didn't necessarily want to be the leader. But he was the leader of the team because of the way he played the game. I've seen the same thing happen with sales groups within a corporate environment.

As a leader, you obviously want to know what's expected of you from your team, but perhaps it's just as important to know what's expected of you from the executive level.

In the corporate environment, I talk about leadership as being from the CEO and the director level not because I think those folks are necessarily leaders. I think they can create an environment so that the leaders can lead and positive expectations are conveyed. And to really enable leadership at every level in an organization, the executives need to let the leaders play the game. Leaders are not developed through micromanagement. Leaders are developed by being given tasks to execute. And they're rewarded for that. Everybody needs to be rewarded for what they do, not necessarily in a grand way but they need some form of recognition.

I recently worked with one person who was an owner of several automobile dealerships in the state of Kentucky. He had called me because he had gotten to the point in his career that his expectations were no longer positive. He would come to work every day and run the company, but he wasn't getting any fulfillment from it. The dealerships were doing well. The salespeople were doing well. He bought a new dealership, and he hoped that would rekindle his emotional flame, but it hadn't done that.

We met several times and talked about a lot of things. We talked about his goals and about how he had inherited the company—we talked about all kinds of things that were peripheral to his work. And it became evident that he had depended on the job to provide him with the fulfillment that should have come from his personal life.

Too many times when I talk with people about expectations, I find that they very seldom talk about personal or family things. Ninety percent of what they list regarding expectations concerns work-related things. And I think it's so important, especially for leaders of a group in a company, to convey what they need to expect success in their personal and professional lives. It really bothered me that he didn't include a single expectation about his personal life. We talked and talked about it, and finally I said, "You know, your job is what you do. It's not who you are."

It's hard to convince young corporate people of that sometimes, but jobs come and go. When it's all said and done, family is all you've got. And you got to understand that you need to have strong, solid expectations in regard to your personal life so that when disappointments come professionally, you can go to your personal life and realize that there are a lot of positive things that are there because you've expected them.

It's very important that when you do your lists you include personal things. I'm not saying that everybody has to be married and have children and go to church. I'm just saying that for every work-related thing that's significant to you, you need to have something personally significant, meaning that your personal, not professional, life needs to be the reason you do what you do. Your job needs to support your personal life. Once you get to that point, then you understand the role of the professional environment within your personal life and you're able to accept the ups and downs a little more easily because the personal things in your life are good and they're consistent.

I've known too many people in sport and in the corporate environment who, when their professional career ended, they were completely lost. And it's sad to see. I've known people who have made hundreds of millions of dollars in their professional lives, but when they don't work anymore and they're with only their personal lives, they're miserable. That's a sad state to be in. You need to make sure that you're always doing things in your professional work to support the personal side of your life.

The only athletes in 45 years that I've ever worried about were those who were lost after they quit playing because they didn't have anything else. I worked with one athlete who had signed his first contract when he was 15. He retired at 73. By the time he was 73, the sport had become his life and when he retired, he had nothing. From the outside looking in, he seemed to have a lot, but within himself he didn't have anything. It's sad to see that happen, but it happens many more times than not. So I work with those people and try to help them understand that you have to keep the wheels turning.

I am 72 and people ask me when I'm going to retire. Why would I retire when I get fulfillment every single day and I expect every day to be a good day? Why would I leave that? And I tell people that I love what I do, I expect good things every day, and I think that's one reason that, as I said before, I've never had a bad day at work in 45 years.

And so you need to be in an environment with at least the potential for excitement every day. There are some jobs that are tougher than others. There are some jobs that are less fulfilling than others. I know that. I'm tuned in to real life. But I also know that many times we let things fall on the negative side of the ledger simply because we don't expect good things to happen. From this point on in the book we'll deal the work environment, stress, and the peripheral things around your job that enable you to be a positive person.

It really bothers me when I see people spend so much money going to hear motivational speakers who scream and holler at them to "pull your own strings" and "reach for the power within." I think people feel good after those meetings for about an hour or so, but then they get back to the job and think, "That speaker has never been in my environment." You need to have long-lasting things that you can hang your hat on. A quick rah-rah meeting or an empty motivational speech is not going to do it.

I have never in 45 years tried to motivate an athlete because, I think, if they're not motivated to play a great game, then they've got issues I can't deal with. It's a privilege, it's a blessing to be able to play sports, and I feel the same way about being in some corporate environments. What an opportunity is the possibility to do well! The team and environment around you play major roles, as we will discuss in later chapters, but you cannot thrive unless you expect to do well every day. Understanding that can be a turning point in your life. If you write your expectations down and look at them every day, it can change your life.

Final Thought

Expect good things to happen,
personally and professionally.

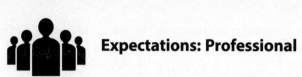 **Expectations: Professional**

Use this worksheet for listing expectations to help to help you win every day as a leader.

List five professional expectations you have for yourself.

1. _____
2. _____
3. _____
4. _____
5. _____

List five things your team expects from you professionally.

1. _____
2. _____
3. _____
4. _____
5. _____

Actions to Meet Professional Expectations

1. _____
2. _____
3. _____
4. _____
5. _____
6. _____
7. _____
8. _____
9. _____
10. _____
11. _____
12. _____
13. _____
14. _____
15. _____

Expectations and Leadership

 **Expectations: Personal**

Use this worksheet for listing expectations to help you win every day.

List five personal expectations you have for yourself.

1. _____
2. _____
3. _____
4. _____
5. _____

List five things others expect from you personally.

1. _____
2. _____
3. _____
4. _____
5. _____

Actions to Meet Personal Expectations

1. _____
2. _____
3. _____
4. _____
5. _____
6. _____
7. _____
8. _____
9. _____
10. _____
11. _____
12. _____
13. _____
14. _____
15. _____

Chapter 6

Teamwork

Once your goals and expectations are determined, leaders choose team members who can help achieve goals. Leaders guide team members and respect their input, and real leaders lead through performance. As an example, over the past several years I've had more requests to give speeches dealing with teamwork than probably any other topic. I've never liked to talk about team building because once a company gets to the point where they invite me, the team is already built. Everybody has a contract and a uniform, so at that point we need to talk about teamwork.

The idea of teamwork is huge. Everywhere you look, everybody—corporations, schools, nonprofits—refers to teams in one way or another. Winners and leaders recognize the importance of the team concept. Leaders know they need to not only be team members but also support the team and be supported by the team members. Leaders need to be sure team members know where they fit and understand their roles on the team. The biggest barrier to realizing the value of a team is a lack of clearly defined roles. As we've discussed before, the reason most people give when they leave a company is that they don't know what's expected; that is, they don't know or understand their role on the team. A lot of people whom you would like to have on your team may be willing, but in order for them to be effective, you need to have a conversation about expectations, roles, and the things that are important to you and your vision.

As you prepare your team for winning every day, you as a leader need to describe where you want to go and what you want to accomplish. Once you've communicated this information, then you need other team members to complement and support your talents. At the same time you, as a leader, need to support the talents of your team members. It's crucial to the team's success and, therefore, to your own.

If your team has only point guards, for example, then all you do is pass the ball around and nobody scores. In other words, if team members are there only to support you and never to challenge you, then you don't accomplish very much. If your team has only shooters, then there's nobody to throw the ball in. You lose either way.

On your team you need both leaders and supporters. You need people who are going to take risks and people who are going to support the risk takers. Sometimes you have to do both. As a leader, you need to be the person to step out front. If you need to do both, as a leader you need to show your team members that you're willing to do whatever it takes to make them successful.

Every employee must feel *critical* to the team's performance and productivity. Every player needs something to which he or she can be attached to personally, something to which he or she can make a genuine contribution. In sports every player must feel critical to the outcome of the game or to the team's status as a winner. In a family, parents must feel critical to the development of their children.

I have multiple sclerosis (MS). I need every team member to recognize my vision, and I also need every team member to recognize my disabilities and when I need help. Everything we do is a team effort even though many times we feel alone.

Even in individual sports there's always a team involved. There's always a support system. There's always someone who understands the goals and the desired outcomes and then tries to contribute to achieving those goals.

On your team, as a leader, you first need to identify and understand what it is you want to accomplish and whether or not a team is actually necessary or important to reaching your goals. I can't personally think of any situation where a team would not be needed. Then you must determine what the members of your team need and how the role of each person factors into the team's shared accountability and expectations.

On every team, you need go-to players, team members who are reliable and on call for specific circumstances. This includes team members who are supportive and those who are challenging to the leadership.

The process of forming your team basically requires you to: number one, evaluate your goals; number two, review your assets and liabilities; and three, make sure that you have not only team members who support your assets but also team members who offset your liabilities. You need to determine the team talents that are needed. You also need to select additional team members with necessary assets. Lastly, you need to select team members who are committed to helping you as a leader.

The most important factor of a team is to make sure that it functions properly. Team members' participation peaks at different times based on the team's needs. Of course, everyone is available when needed.

Remember that it takes only one individual to cause the team to lose. Have you ever observed a situation where everyone has a good attitude, then one negative person walks in and within 15 minutes the whole team is down? You have to separate yourself and your colleagues from that kind of a team wrecker. Eliminating such a person's presence will automatically improve the probability that your team will succeed. As a leader it's a very interesting situation to be in because you want everybody to be successful. Even if a leader has a caring and supportive attitude, there are times when the environment is not right for certain people. It doesn't mean they're bad people or incompetent;

it just means they don't fit with the environment. The chemistry's not there. And with that said, those people need to find a new environment so leaders can preserve the attitude of the positive team members who are left.

You know the cliché that is very appropriate here: It takes only one rotten apple to spoil the whole bushel. I remember one person I worked with a few years ago who had several team members who supported what she did and what she wanted to accomplish. Then, almost overnight, one team member decided to take control and do what she thought was best for the whole team. As opposed to being a support person, she took on the role of being the leader and made everything all about her. It didn't take long for the team to become disrupted and very dysfunctional.

My advice was really simple and commonsense: Eliminate that person from the team. It doesn't mean she's a bad person. It doesn't mean that she didn't have good intentions. But, in this case, it meant that she didn't fit in that particular team concept. Once she was eliminated, the team came back together, and the person who had established it as a support system became very successful.

When you forge your team, what you should put in place is something that will be enduring and present every day. People will see it, feel it, and want to be a part of it. This intangible quality should remain even if you make changes. In other words, the team concept is an enduring factor. It needs to be related to your philosophy of a team, your goals for your team, and the foundation of the team. It must be capable of living through even the most dramatic changes a team could face. The winning chemistry of the team must be constant because it will be based on the same basic philosophy that you had when you started.

This foundational concept should be what keeps the engine running smoothly. Now, changes on the team are something natural. They are not always comfortable, but they need to be made on occasion for the good of the whole team. Change can be exciting and it can be rewarding. Variation of the team's makeup can produce tremendous results if it's done for the right reasons and the goals are kept paramount. In teams and in families, you must have dramatic changes like those that occur in sports.

There are still times that will test your team philosophy, but if the basic concepts are what they should be, then you must hold onto them, keep them out front, and strive toward your goals every day without fail. You must be able to call on team members when they veer off track so then you're in a winning mode.

In almost every team, whether it's personal or professional, there are going to be conflicts. To be a winning team does not mean that team members have to love each other. It means that they have to respect each other's assets and liabilities and they have to play in a coordinated way. Conflicts are part of the equation, and in many cases they make a team stronger, especially when they're resolved. Conflict can be a positive thing if it causes change and risk taking, which are good for the team.

Recognition of the contribution of the team members is essential. As a leader, you need to be in a position to provide recognition for team members when they make significant contributions. They're going to look to you for support, they'll look to you for positive reinforcement, and you need to deliver that. That's one of the areas in which we don't do a very good job in the corporate environment. We're quick to point out mistakes and very slow to point out the good things that people do. It's very important that when team members do things for the good of the team—things that may challenge you or that you might initially disagree with—it's very important that you recognize those contributions. It's true for every kind of team, whether it's a personal team, family team, or corporate team. Let me give a good example that I've used many times, and have probably used in every book that I've written, of what I consider to be consummate team concepts.

When I spoke at a company's annual employee-appreciation meeting around the year 2000, it was neat to see everybody in the corporate structure come to the meeting. The cleanup up crews, the gardeners, and the receptionists sat at the same tables and had lunch with the corporate people. I had refused to speak at the meeting if they didn't invite those people because I thought they were very important team members. It was interesting to hear one member of the janitorial staff tell me it was the first time in 25 years he'd had lunch with one of the corporate members. They got to know each other and became friends. It was one of the most enjoyable professional experiences I have had.

Talking with those team members and watching them interact, I could easily see that they shared a strongly coordinated work ethic and common goals. That environment was what I consider to be a winning chemistry. Chemistry is one of the areas that we play down in the corporate environment because you can't attach numbers to it and profit from it directly. But it is an absolutely critical concept to be nurtured by team leaders. If you do nothing else in your environment with your team, improve its chemistry and coordination. Then you've done your job.

Here's another example. I was working with a sports team in which the chemistry was never emphasized. The team was made up of talented athletes, but it was not a true team. There were no support players. The players were a group of individuals who played under a team name, and they were not successful.

To give you an example, they had a player on the team who was voted MVP of the league but he probably did more to compromise other players than anyone else on the team. He was such an incredibly selfish individual that he may have played great and produced his own great numbers, but he likely cost his team a chance at success because of how he disrupted the chemistry in the dressing room.

Chemistry is one of those things that we don't talk about until we don't have it. On your team you need some members who are supporting players. You also need others who are independent, adventurous, aggressive, risk-taking, and those who want to be in control. To make it the consummate team, you need diversity, so the team can't consist of only your friends; it needs people who are going to enable you to be successful.

I've always said that the consummate coach is the one who creates an environment that has good chemistry in which the players can play the game. I was with the Atlanta Braves for 16 years, and I always admired their manager, Bobby Cox, because he only had two rules: Show up early and play hard. He put the names on the lineup, and he let the players play. He was very smart in how he did that, and he also put them in positions where they could succeed. One of the things that he did that I admired most was that he let the leaders lead.

As I said in the first chapter of this book, the leaders are not the CEOs, the managers, and the coaches. The leaders are the players. The leaders are everyday guys on the team. Bobby always let that happen and therefore we won a record 14 consecutive division titles, which will probably never be broken. We were able to do that because every single year, even though sometimes we would have 10 to 12 new players on the 25-man roster, we kept our leadership players, and everything seemed to fall in place. The chemistry was good. Every year, those leaders who played every day made sure that the chemistry stayed good, and it was obviously a prescription for success.

I like to use a very specific personal example of the importance of leaders within a team. Since I was diagnosed with MS a few years ago, I established what I think of as a team that has enabled me to stay relatively healthy and also to remain productive. When you're diagnosed with a devastating disease for which there's no cure, it's very easy to be emotionally down. It's easy to crawl into a hole and avoid contact with people. But early on, right after I was diagnosed, I established my team because my doctor had told me that, no matter what medication we picked, my attitude would to be my best friend or my worst enemy for the rest of my life. Everybody needs a team that's good for them.

My team members may seem unusual, but they're good for me. One of the people I chose for my team was Bobby Cox. He was not only supportive during the four or five years I stayed with the Braves after my diagnosis, but he also had a way of creating an environment where the emphasis was not on the downside of my illness. People often accuse me of making fun of MS, but that isn't the case. I accept it for what it is, and so did everybody around me on the Atlanta Braves. Bobby was very compassionate, very caring, but at the same time, as I've always told people, he was the captain of my team because he never once in those four or five years excused me from doing my job. And even though he has a very strong compassionate side, he understood what I needed to do. That may sound strange to some, but it's very effective for me because it kept my wheels turning. I had so much respect for him that there was no way I would not do the job that I was hired to do. It was just understood that was the way it was supposed to be. I had occasions where I couldn't go to the stadium or didn't feel good or it was too hot. I could have called and said, "You know, I'm not coming," and he could have said, "That's fine," but he didn't do that. I credit him for keeping me in a healthy state of mind.

One of my other team members was Ben Thrower, a neurologist at the Shepherd Spinal Center in Atlanta. He's my physician and I trust him with my life. People ask me what medications I take, and I have no idea what some of them are, but Dr. Thrower prescribed them, so I take them. Everybody should have somebody they trust in that way. I never question what he says to me or what he recommends to me. He's a very important team member.

I have other team members as well. My children are the reason I continue to do what I do. They are my inspiration, and I consider them to be critical team members. I have friends on my team who call me constantly and check on my health and see how I'm doing, and I tell them I'm hanging in there. Then I have other team members who are friends and challenge me on a daily or weekly basis. When I say to them, "I don't think I can go to lunch," their response is, "Be ready in 15 minutes. We're going to lunch." I always feel better after I do those things.

As I mentioned before, it would be very easy to feel bad, and it's so difficult sometimes to feel good. But once you take the step to feel better—and sometimes it takes team members to cause you to take that step—then you're glad you took the risk and also glad you took the chance.

I think one of the most critical requirements with team members is that you, as the leader, need team members who actually talk to you. We need to move away from Facebooking, texting, Twittering, and e-mailing. We need to communicate at least verbally, if not face to face. It's very important that you realize that 60 percent of communication is nonverbal. It's virtually impossible to use that 60 percent if you're texting or e-mailing. You need to physically see people. You need to be able to read people. We've used the cliché a few times in this book: *What you are talks so loud people can't hear what you say.* Basically that means that people need to see you, see your reactions, see your eyes, see your body, see your posture, see how well you're moving around. They need to feel those things and good team members are willing to do that.

As a leader, it's very important that you promote face-to-face communication. We've gotten away from talking. We are raising generations of socially awkward kids because they don't talk anymore. And the further we move away from that, then the more isolated we become as members of a team. It's your job, as the leader, to change this situation if you see it happening. It's very important that people respect what you're trying to do in regard to communication because that's such a big part of leadership.

In regard to communication, one of the most important things you can convey to your team members is that it's critical to address issues right away. If you have a problem on Monday, don't call me on Thursday to tell me about it because I don't care. But if you have a problem on Monday and you call me Monday, I care a whole lot. And so you need to make sure that everything is up to the minute and up to date in regard to basic communication. It's not hard. I know when things get tough, common sense is the first thing to go, but common-sense leadership is communicating with your people, reading their body language, and making sure that you keep those folks on track.

In a corporate environment, you can always conjure up ideas about how to make your team better, but I think the consummate team starts with the environment. I've been in both sport and the corporate environment; both are like a NASCAR pit crew. It's amazing to me that when a car comes into the pit, there are five people who are called *over-the-wall people*. These five people change four tires, fill the car with gas, pull off the windshield liner, get the debris off the grill, make adjustments to the car, and give some water to the driver—doing it all in 11 seconds. And they practice every single day. When I used to go to the NASCAR shop for the team I was working with, I'd go out back and watch them practice. They would have a guy driving the car. He would pull up and the pit guys would do what they do. They'd change little things and tweak the process to save the guys a half step or enable them to make a quicker turn around the car, or to help the jack man get there faster. I mean, it's amazing when you think about it to watch them do what they do.

When I was working with Tony Stewart's pit crew in 2002, they would get a huge bonus if they completed everything in less than 13 seconds—so they wound up being able to do it in 11 seconds. It's just incredible, the coordination of the team. At the track, they have computers that track the amount of gas a car has and how far it will take you; it's accurate up to half a lap. Drivers will call to the pit crew or to the crew chief and say, "I need a quarter pound of air taken out of the back right tire." Meanwhile, I'm sitting here thinking I barely know when my tire's flat. But it's something that they've learned to do through years of practice and training. NASCAR pit crews display some of the best-coordinated team effort that I've ever seen, and if you ever get a chance to see it, even if it's on TV, it will do you and your team some good to watch it.

We could talk about teamwork for days, and everyone can always come up with several examples of good teamwork versus bad teamwork. But the important thing to remember as the team leader is that it's your responsibility to ensure that the team works smoothly. It's your responsibility to help people be in the right spots at the right time. It's your responsibility to coach upward so that people above you understand what you're doing as a team leader.

In summary, I think it's important to: number one, recognize your assets and your liabilities; number two, select team members who offset your liabilities and other members who supplement your assets; number three, select team members who are committed to helping you reach your goals; and number four, communicate your goals and aspirations to team members so that they understand what you expect from them.

And it's not a bad idea to talk with the team every single day about how important this all is because some folks are not going to listen all the time. That's just life as it is. So, we need to make sure as leaders that we keep team concepts out front every single day because that increases productivity and confidence and really eliminates basic paranoia in the job environment.

The final key to teamwork is that leaders need to recognize team members when they do something for you. It takes nothing more than a comment many times to show how valuable it is when team members try to do their best to make life better for the team. You need to recognize those people on your team. It may be weekly. It may be monthly. It may be yearly. But at your discretion, you have to get your team together and recognize everyone around the table for their contributions, which enable you to become more successful.

I would like nothing better than to be able to have all my team members get together so we could sit down face to face and I could recognize all of them. That's not possible, but it doesn't mean that we're not a team. We may be spread all over the world, but I know that the ones who don't live close to me are only a phone call away, and that's a great feeling. If you decide that you need a team, which I think everybody does, then you also need to make the commitment to have the team help you. This is no truer than in the corporate environment. You have people who really want to do well. Sometimes they disguise it, but they want to accomplish things. All they're looking for is recognition and some specific expectations. With that, they'll be a strong team for you; and you, as a leader, influence their behaviors every single day.

Final Thought

Respect your team members' talents.

 **Personal Team Structure**

Talents/Assets Needed

1. _____
2. _____
3. _____
4. _____
5. _____

Players Needed

1. _____
2. _____
3. _____
4. _____
5. _____

 **Professional Team Structure**

Talents/Assets Needed

1. _____
2. _____
3. _____
4. _____
5. _____

Players Needed

1. _____
2. _____
3. _____
4. _____
5. _____

 **Know Your Team**

What is expected of me as a team member? What do I bring to the mix?

    1. _____

    2. _____

    3. _____

    4. _____

What is our team personality?

    1. _____

    2. _____

    3. _____

    4. _____

What are the team's goals and what do they mean to me?

    1. _____

    2. _____

    3. _____

    4. _____

What resources are available to reach our goals?

    1. _____

    2. _____

    3. _____

    4. _____

    5. _____

What happens when we reach our goal as a team?

1. _____
2. _____
3. _____
4. _____
5. _____

Chapter 7

Creating a Positive Work Environment

O ne of the most important responsibilities of a leader is to help create a positive work environment. This may be the most critical factor in succeeding and, at the same time, one of the most neglected factors in productivity. It's also one of the most vital determinates of performance outcome, and it's a factor that leaders can influence immediately.

How many times have poorly performing athletes been traded to different teams only to become high-level performers? Several cases of this worst-to-first scenario have occurred every year in professional baseball as well as in other sports over the past 10 to 15 years. Baseball players struggling with offense have gone to another team and raised their battling average as much as 50 or 60 points. There may be some influence from different managers, coaches, and stadiums, but the determining factor is probably the change in environment.

The same thing happens in the corporate environment, where some people perform at a very average level and then, when they're moved to a different office, city, or region on the same team, they become much better performers. This is an environmental factor without question.

Look at almost any new sports stadium, and you'll find a tremendous difference in the environment provided for the home team as opposed to the one provided for the visiting team. If you've never been in the belly of a stadium, you probably don't realize this, but in most stadiums, regardless of the sport, the visiting team is afforded very poor

93

environmental conditions as opposed to the home team. It's always been that way and probably always will be. The differences range from the color of the walls to the size of the space to the amenities—all environmental factors. And the same holds true in the business environment, in schools, and even in the home.

It's most evident, I think, in the educational environment when you go into different schools and even different classrooms. It's very revealing how cold some classrooms are and how warm others are. I remember going into my second grader's classroom on Parents' Night, looking around, and telling the teacher, "I don't blame my son for not wanting to be here because this is the coldest, stalest environment I think I've ever been in. It's not motivating, it's not exciting, and so the brighter kids especially are not going to perform well here."

The environment is fascinating because it is present every day, and it encompasses not only the physical surroundings but also the psychological components and the people who are part of it. A lot of money and time are spent motivating people, only to send them back into the same negative environment. (In Chapter 10 we will talk about motivation and the environment.)

How do you create a motivating environment? How do you enhance the environment in such a way that motivated people want to be there?

You need to be able to read the environment. How do you read it? How do you walk in and determine if the environment is positive, neutral, or negative? How do you evaluate the physical properties in the environment? Psychology students are taught to look at the furniture, the wall colors, the pictures, decor, and other things when they go into an office. They read the environment and learn something about the people in it. They look for *psychological noise.*

What is psychological noise? It is a critical factor in the environment, especially in the corporate setting, and there are various ways that noise can play a role. For example, baseball fans made much of the physical environment in the Minneapolis Metrodome with regard to the outcome of the World Series between the Minnesota Twins and the Atlanta Braves in 1991. The environmental factors at play were the noise; the white hankies every person in every seat was waving the whole time; the dome's white ceiling, which made it hard for fielders to see fly balls; and the very closed-in nature of the stadium. And there were rumors that when the Braves were hitting, the air conditioning was blowing in and when the Twins were up, the air conditioning was turned off. I don't know that that's true; it's just a rumor. Even so, the environment obviously constituted a tremendous home-field advantage for Minnesota, but it posed a serious disadvantage to the visiting team. All the distractions might well have influenced the outcome of the series, which the Twins won.

To look at an entirely different industry, restaurants may use fast music to turn tables faster if they depend on a high table turn. A high-ticket restaurant with low table turn ratio may play slower music so people can sit and relax. Bars that depend on a high percentage of alcohol sales will play faster music, which means people tend to drink faster. Piano bars where selling a lot of alcohol is not a priority will play slower music. These are all forms of psychological noise.

Other examples are evident in the sporting events that we attend. Cameras flashing can cause distraction. In fact, one click of a camera can throw a golfer's swing out of sync, which will cause bad shots and even bad tournaments. I've never understood this. I've always thought that if you're focused, then you don't hear that noise, but it's a matter of what you're used to. If you have watched a World Series game, you know that with every pitch and every swing of the bat, there are camera flashes all over the stadium. Unless players are conditioned so the disruptions blend into the background, cameras and flashes constitute psychological noise in the environment.

I feel very strongly that a positive environment equals record productivity. One of my corporate clients makes over 300 million pounds of french fries a year. They asked me to come in to talk to their employees at a plant located in a small town in a desert area in the Northwest. Once a month I visited the plant and worked with the people there trying to create teamwork and to develop management. I wanted to get a feel for what they did, so I went into the plant and worked two 12-hour shifts back to back. That told me what I wanted to know about the environment. It was not stimulating. It was depressing and extremely monotonous. Over a year's time, making monthly evaluations, I saw no real change, and I learned that the employees had become so conditioned to the environment that it did not rate as a concern to them. When new people came in, they did not perform well and were not very productive. But the people who lived in the town, most of whom worked in the plant, were conditioned to it. From the outside, I saw a deadening environment, but the perception from the inside was that the job was a way to make a living; it was what they needed to do to survive.

The executives of the company did not live in the town but rather in a large city a considerable distance away. Clearly they were not tuned in to the culture of the plant. They didn't understand the issues and therefore felt no need to make changes so long as production remained at an acceptable level. Yet production could have been maintained and, at the same time, the employees could have enjoyed their work and had more fulfilling personal lives if the company had embraced the changes that were proposed in my program.

I had suggested that they start recognizing good performance in the workforce with rewards such as time off, gift certificates to the one restaurant in the town, or some pretty cool gifts; it should be the winner's choice. I also wanted to get a jogging track around the plant with some recreational equipment to be used during break time. In addition, I felt that someone in the workforce should be on the management council. I suggested a process evaluation similar to the one that I had conducted at a hazardous waste plant (Chapter 4). The program wouldn't have been magic. It followed common sense to signal that ownership cared about the people in the plant, but the changes were never made.

You see, when things are tough, we try to get creative and we try to do these nifty hot-shot programs, but what we should be following is common sense. It's common sense that the leaders need to take control in this environment and pass the word along to management. It's common sense that they need to observe every single day that there are some things that can make the environment better. So 300 million pounds of french fries a month is good, but what if they could do 325 or 350 or 400 million pounds per month. Would that not be better? And with some minor adjustments to the environment, they could have more fun and spend less energy doing the same work, which would show that the company cared about its people.

If you're going to influence the environment in the workplace, you need to do something more than a short-term motivational session and a once-a-month visit as those executives did. You need to be a part of the environment so you can feel it, you can experience it, and you can understand what people go through on a daily basis. Only then are you prepared to make productive changes. When management is thousands of miles away from the work environment, the primary local leader has much more influence on what goes on inside. Leaders need to take advantage of that.

Not too long ago, corporations went through a phase of having employees take *ownership* of their respective jobs. The term became overused and went the way of *quality* and *excellence* and those other buzzwords. I was called in to give guidance for a company that asked its employees to take *ownership* in a plant environment that was not clean, lacked areas for employees to take a break, and had no restrooms.

When I met with the administrator, I suggested we try something different. Instead of trying to motivate the employees to take ownership

Creating a Positive Work Environment

of something that I certainly would not want to take ownership of, why not try to create an environment that they would enjoy being in?

People are not likely to buy into something that is not appealing to them. I think the most valuable investment that a company or a team or a parent can make is to provide an attractive environment so the key players want to be there. Again, a tremendous amount of money is spent on motivation and motivational speakers when that money could be spent more effectively in creating a positive environment. It's self-defeating to motivate people and send them back into a negative environment. Motivational sessions can be effective over the short term, for a number of hours, but if you're looking long term, the environmental issues will probably shape the productivity curve in most endeavors, personal or professional.

As I mentioned before, I've been in educational environments that were incredibly cold, uninviting, and demotivating, but the teachers can't understand why the children don't learn. If a school environment is cold and not family oriented—for example, an environment that resents family members visiting their children at school or joining them for lunch—then you've got a formula for failure.

Compare that to another school that invites family participation. The administrators prefer a social atmosphere for the learning process. The teachers are involved with the students and welcome input and feedback from the parents. Doesn't that sound like a much healthier environment for children? It's an incentive to learn. It's the kind of place that may make you wonder why there wasn't any place like it when you were in school.

At least some companies in the business world are learning the lesson. I know a sports marketing company that owes much of its success to a minor but extremely important practice. When an employee is not performing well, the owner of the business does everything possible to put that person in an environment where he or she can succeed. Instead of just firing the employee in whom the company has already made an investment, the owner first tries to solve the problem by modifying the worker's environment. It makes good business sense, and it's also humane.

Enjoying your work and seeking to please customers rank as the top priorities when creating or modifying the environment for positive results. This fact struck me when I worked with another restaurant company. Again, as a way of preparing for the challenge, I worked in the restaurant for a week trying to get a feel for how people felt about their jobs. It was fascinating. I worked in the kitchen, where I discovered that those employees were very proud of what they did. Surprisingly, they became very protective of their specific jobs. If I tried to help them do something at first, I was rejected because the employees took a great deal of pride in what they did. It was their job, they wanted it done right, and they didn't want to give up any part of it. Several days went by before any of them let me do anything other than sweep the floor. That business proved to be very successful because the management promoted an environment that encouraged people to enjoy their work, which resulted in the customers enjoying their dining experiences and returning again and again.

While working with one university fast-pitch softball team, I noticed that before and after every game every player had an assignment to help maintain the quality of the field, such as dragging the infield, raking the pitcher's mound, or cutting the grass. Everyone had a specific job they did before the game, and they would do it again after the game. When I asked the coach why he did this, he told me that players take more pride in the field and the game when they're responsible for taking care of the environment. That made a lot of sense. It also makes a ton of sense for a corporate environment, and leaders are the people who need to recognize this and make little changes to the environment so workers are more productive.

People tend to neglect so many aspects that are environmentally related, but it's something everyone should spend some time thinking

Creating a Positive Work Environment

about. It's amazing that so many people look around their environment but don't even notice what's important. Consequently, they don't learn anything. When you're in an environment, whether it's at home or school, or in a business or a sports setting, you should be able to look around and learn how to manipulate the environment, if necessary, in order to facilitate the enterprise and move to the next level.

I've always recommended that we need to spend time looking at peripheral things in order to learn what's best about our environment. When did you last go to a playground and watch children play? They create games. They make up rules. Then they play the game. They reach an outcome and they go home. Remember some of the creative things you did when you were 8 or 10 years old? Most of these were facilitated or even determined by the environment. Perhaps a lack of resources or equipment caused you to be creative with your environment. The results may have been off the wall in a grown-up's world but now you see them as creative.

For example, did you ever play sock ball using a broom handle as a bat? Our rule was that if you hit the sock over the house it was a home run. If the sock stayed on the roof, the game was over. And if the sock got worn out, some more folks took their socks off, made another sock ball, and kept playing.

A favorite question of mine at every convention is how many of you here today are as creative as you were when you were children. Many times no hands are raised. Yet the truth is that everyone is as creative today as when they were children. It's just that when we become adults, the size of the box gets smaller, we get more reserved, and we don't want to say creative things because people around us might think that we're strange. Stop and think how many millions of dollars have been made on such goofy, childlike ideas as Hula-Hoops and Beanie Babies and Pet Rocks, yet people as a general rule tend to be more and more content to survive on the traditional way of doing things. In fact, we surround ourselves with things in the environment, whether it's personally or professionally, that basically curtail our creativity, things that make it so easy that all we have to do is push a button to get something done. We don't have to do creative things to be successful, so we stifle any ideas we might have that would make us more visible, make us more accountable, and make us obviously a lot better at what we do.

It seems to me that creativity is nothing more than unused common sense. It's just sitting in there waiting to jump out. Commonsense things that kids do, for example, are often very creative ways to negotiate better, settle arguments, deal with conflict, engage in wholesome competition, play to win, and recover from adversity. If you have ever seen children get in a fight on a playground, you know that unless an adult steps in and messes up the whole deal, the kids get over it and go get a sandwich. But if adult gets involved, it's a prolonged issue for days; it gets to the teacher level and then even to the parent level.

The creativity and positive impact of children on the environment struck me once on a trip with the family to our beach house on the Gulf Coast of Florida. The house had been impacted by a storm and was rebuilt board by board. By the time we arrived, we had to do a lot of painting. I was upstairs painting when my six-year-old daughter came into the room and announced to me that we were going to play school.

"You're my student, and your name is Lloyd," she told me.

I said, "Fine," and went on with my painting. And she left the room and I thought it was over.

Well, a couple of minutes go by, the door flies open, and she runs in the room and says, "Okay, Lloyd, I've had enough of your lip. I'm going to call your mama. You're in time out." There I was, 54 years old and sitting in a corner, painting a little spot, because I'm in time out and didn't want to get in any more trouble.

If you're a parent, you know what it's like to find yourself as a part of your children's environment creativity. It's great fun. We need to facilitate that more in children, but an even greater need is to facilitate

Creating a Positive Work Environment

this creativity in adults in the corporate environment and in the world around us.

If children are at one end of the environment spectrum, older folks are at the other end. They're an equally neglected learning resource. I don't know why when people get to be 60 or 65, corporations seem to think that they can kick them out without having a negative effect on the environment. It's not that businesses don't need young energy coming into the corporate environment—they do. But we have an invaluable resource in older people who have experience—maybe not in technology or related skills—but in the corporate culture. Their knowledge and experience are fundamental components of the corporate environment. And obviously, the longer they've been around, the more they have to contribute along these lines.

I recently attended a convention for a large retail industry when I asked the audience this question, "Wouldn't it be fun to have a panel of former retail people who had spent their whole careers in the retail industry? We could put people who were 85 and 90 on the panel and ask them questions about how they sold their products and how they did different things in the environment without the technology we have." As I told these retailers, I think it would be a tremendous learning experience for young people. We just can't keep putting people out to pasture. I've learned most of life's important lessons from older people.

My grandfather was a good example of how an elderly person can contribute to the environment, broadly defined as the space in which we live and learn. I learned more from him about why I do what I do than I learned in 22 years of school. He was a welder on the railroad for 45 years and when he fixed the nicks on the rails, the train tracks were safer. You're probably wondering what would motivate a person to do this for 45 years, move from one nick in the rail to the next. The answer is dignity and work and pride in doing a job well. Because my grandfather constituted an essential part of my environment as I grew up, he communicated those important values to me.

I'm not sure you can teach that in seminars. I'm not sure you can learn it in school. I think it's there inside. You do something that's fulfilling and you understand the true reason why you do it, then you begin to have a level of pride, not only in what you do but maybe more importantly in who you are. These are the sorts of lessons that you absorb from a healthy environment. They don't need to be in the books you read. They're in the air you breathe.

If you know somebody 90 or 100 years old, you need to sit and talk with that person. I will guarantee that afterwards you will know something you didn't know before. You might even begin to know why you do what you do. We need to rethink the role that our older folks play creating and maintaining the environment around us. I'm not sure there's a better teaching tool in the world for learning how to deal with people and how to lead and follow.

My mom worked full time for most of her life, starting when she was 16 years old, and she always worked around young people. At 82, when she quit—or was asked to quit— I asked her why she left her job.

She said, "These young girls, all they talk about is computer, computer, computer." My mom was a file kind of person and she just couldn't make that transition to computer files and digital information storage. But she was very popular in the workplace. When the younger workers had issues, whether on the job or personally, they went to my mom. And that made her feel very worthwhile and wanted and productive. And it was interesting that within six months of leaving her job, she developed the early signs of Alzheimer's disease. I think that happened because the wheels quit turning. Since I've been diagnosed with multiple sclerosis (MS), after 30 minutes of FreeCell or solitaire on my computer in the morning, I can tell you what kind of day I'm going to have, whether or not the wheels are going to turn as they should.

Now, leaders are people who can recognize the cognitive factors that influence the different people in the work force. They are the people who can put you in an environment where you can get the wheels started and keep them turning and be productive and enjoy your life and use less energy doing it. The environment is without question a leadership tool that can be changed every day. If necessary, it can be altered in some way that makes it more conducive to having people be productive.

If you look back at older research in psychology, there are studies that indicate that when offices raise the lighting level, productivity goes up. In another study, a company painted the walls so each worker would be surrounded by his or her favorite color. Then, they put up pictures of things the workers had said they liked. When the office staff returned to the new space, productivity increased, without the workers noticing a difference in their effort level. In summary, what this means is that people want to feel appreciated and that the people at the executive level care about them. This change starts with the leader creating that environment, creating some psychological noise that's favorable to productivity.

Final Thought

Create a positive environment for your team and let them play.

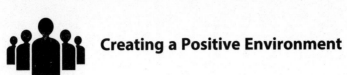

Creating a Positive Environment

List the things *you can do* to enhance the work environment for your team.

1. _____
2. _____
3. _____
4. _____
5. _____
6. _____
7. _____
8. _____
9. _____
10. _____

List the things *you can do* to enhance your personal environment.

1. _____
2. _____
3. _____
4. _____
5. _____
6. _____
7. _____
8. _____
9. _____
10. _____

Creating a Positive Work Environment

Chapter 8

Leading Your Team from Habitual to Perceptual Behaviors

L eaders help the workforce to replace habitual behaviors with perceptual behaviors. It's not a topic that's often discussed in leadership books but it's very important. This is not an easy task but it is critical to recovering from adversity more quickly. At a very early age, individuals learn basic habits that are necessary to move through life's challenges. A complete list of habits is, of course, beyond the scope of this chapter.

Habitual behavior is using conditioned responses without regard to environmental factors that we consider psychological noise. In children, habits begin as basic reflexes and progress to conditioned reflexes such as walking, running, throwing, and catching. Extracurricular activities provide an environment for refining these particular habits. Classrooms enable students to develop good study habits. Cultural surroundings provide learning opportunities for behavioral and social habits.

People are constantly bombarded with talk about the need to have good habits. Every time you go to a corporate meeting, there's at least one session on executing habits, which is a good topic but can be overemphasized. There have been a number of programs on the habits of successful people, the most famous example coming from Stephen Covey's book *The Seven Habits of Highly Effective People*. I know there are many more habits than that, and as people progress in the corporate world they begin to analyze which ones are necessary for performance.

Habits become ingrained in young people through a process similar to the memorization of facts. Through repetition, students can internalize knowledge, then they regurgitate those facts to score well on tests, make good grades—and consequently develop a false sense of security, which leaves them ill-prepared for a successful life, both personally and professionally. Education has become an environment for teaching to the test as opposed to teaching skills that are going to help children throughout their lives. As a result, people become conditioned to hanging their potential for success on the execution of correct habits, a very dangerous precedent to set.

In athletics, there are two types of sports, habitual and perceptual. In habitual sports, such as golf, gymnastics, ice-skating, swimming, and bowling, habitual execution will ensure a comfortable level of success. In these sports, an athlete tries to execute conditioned skills, regardless of environmental factors and the skill level of opponents. In the corporate world, salespeople are trained to execute habits like athletes in these sports.

At one recent convention where I was speaking, participants were encouraged to get back to basic habits. Bookstore shelves are packed with books promoting habits of successful people. Readers become conditioned to be habitual and may reach a comfortable level of success through this approach, but they will never really win. Harnessing habits means they are merely surviving at a performance level.

The habitual training that makes me most uncomfortable is that of parents training their children. It's also a bit uncomfortable knowing that many authors of parenting books do not have children of their own. For example, there's a program that appears regularly on TV about how to change your child's behavior in 30 seconds. I think it's obvious that person doesn't have children. I've always thought if you haven't been locked in the basement at least once by your child, you don't know much about parenting.

In many ways, the training espoused by these programs reminds me of Pavlov's dogs: hear the bell and salivate. Parenting is the consummate trial-and-error challenge. In short, habitual performances may enable one to perform, compete, and survive—but not to thrive. As a parent, the more habitual you are, the lower your probability of success.

Relying on habit is probably a good plan if one goes through life free from adversity. The basic flaw in this position is that an adversity-free life is nothing more than a fantasy. I don't say this to minimize the necessity of habitual behavior because habits are, in fact, the very foundation of our journey through life, both personally and professionally. Essentially, the consistent execution of habits only guarantees that people will reach a certain level of performance in all phases of their lives, at which point they will plateau. Progress stops and survival starts. Being a parent of four children, I realized early on that no two children are exactly alike, therefore raising them successfully cannot be accomplished using parental habits learned in classes. The children who are raised by parents to be perceptual in the environment and who learn to make decisions accordingly will mature more quickly and become more productive adults.

When I'm talking with young people, I always use the example of baby birds. If you were raised in the country like I was, you may have watched a bird's nest. We'd hear the baby birds chirping and see the mom come and feed them, and then fly away. After a few days the baby birds get up on the edge of the nest to eat. After another few days of watching the mom fly away, they sit on the edge of the nest and flap their wings. Soon, the birds flap their wings and try to fly, and they fall slowly to the ground. But the mom watches over them to make sure that they're protected while they learn to fly. After a day or so, they'll flap their wings and they'll fly high enough to reach the trees before they fall. And not long after that, you don't see them anymore because they're successfully flying from tree to tree. I've always told people it's virtually impossible to learn to fly between trees unless you've flown into them. In other words, adversity is a part of life. And if you're going to learn to progress and be better, you learn to fly around the trees.

Winners are the people who desire a higher level of existence. Leaders demonstrate the ability to approach every day with the intent of learning more, accomplishing more, and getting more fulfillment from life and from their team. These are the people who use habits as a platform to be perceptual. You can stop here if you're happy being a creature of habit. If you want to achieve more and reach a higher level of performance and fulfillment, then you need to become perceptual. Every day brings the opportunity for a leader to help his or her team members to reach beyond their customary, routine activities. Adversity or, as I call it, *mud in the water*, requires us to use habits to become perceptual.

Now, perceptual behavior is externally focused, attending to environmental factors and then responding with appropriate actions. This feedback loop has the effect of modifying habitual actions.

At this point in the chapter it should be obvious that the more comfortable lifestyle is one of consistent, habitual execution. The basic problem with this hypothesis comes from environmental factors. That psychological noise we discussed in Chapter 7 constantly challenges the success of habits. Those who are comfortable and complacent must find an environment conducive to accepting their habitual lifestyle. That is possible, but it's not likely that such an environment exists.

The alternative is to become so confident in your habits that you can manage and modify them to facilitate performance in a changing environment. These are exciting people, committed to perceptual behavior. Risk takers are those who thrive on stress. These people live on the emotional edge.

Perceptual people use anxiety as an asset as opposed to a liability in performing tasks at hand. It seems that in reviewing the normal life cycle there are at least two determinants to perceptual development.

Several research studies from a few years ago indicated that infants who were sedentary seemed to learn more quickly than those who were active. If this is true, I would suspect that long-term follow-up research would indicate that those children who were active would be better able to apply their knowledge than the more sedentary youngsters.

Knowledge without application and development of habits through mimicry both inhibit perceptual development. Exploring one's environment in combination with knowledge facilitates the learning of life skills, enabling a person to become more perceptual.

When basic habits are not successful, perceptual children are able to modify them to be successful in different environments. This holds true especially in the corporate environment where every day may be different and the same habits will not be successful. So it's very important that a leader help people use their basic habits as a foundation and then learn to be perceptual within the environment.

When I have an opportunity to address teachers, I encourage them to use their expertise, whether it's math, science, art, music, or anything else, to teach children life skills. These skills enable them to get closer to their potential in an ever-changing world and to recover more quickly from unexpected adversity.

Another potential detriment to perceptual development is technology. Technology may be our greatest asset, but it also may become a liability to our development. Education has become more efficient while it has also lost its effectiveness. Too many children are spending more time on their computers and less time being active in their environment. They skip learning basic skills that might lead to perceptual behaviors and instead depend on technology to provide them with everything they need.

In some universities, students are required to have a laptop computer, which enables them to not attend classes. Lecture notes and slides are provided online. This mode of education is very similar to homeschooling, which is a social-development tragedy for children. Many homeschooled athletes with whom I work lack the life skills needed to live in the real world. A large percentage of those students are efficient and intelligent, but they are not prepared to use their knowledge in a perceptual way. Technology could be beneficial to young people if it is *part* of the educational process, but it does not constitute a total solution. The same holds true in a corporate environment. You can go into an office and find that everyone's on the computer; no one's talking and communication suffers dramatically because of technology.

I had a corporate person call me to work with one of his most technically skilled employees who was really struggling in the work environment. He told me she had not talked with her supervisor for three months. When I got there, he showed me where her desk was located. And I asked him, "Where's the supervisor located?" Well, as it turned out, she was probably only three or four feet away in a cubicle. They texted back and forth; they didn't actually talk.

So after work one afternoon, their manager, who had hired me, and I removed the partition between the supervisor and the worker. When they came in the next day, they were surprised they had to sit and look at each other, which forced them to begin communicating verbally. The bottom line was the problem between the two of them was resolved within eight hours. When their habitual reliance on social media was disrupted, their communication became more perceptual because they had to read each other.

The transition from habitual to perceptual behaviors is very clearly observed in sports, making sport participation at any level a valuable experience. Basic behaviors get athletes to a certain level of success, but the top athletes are able to expand habits into perceptual movements. The resulting behavior depends on several factors in the competitive environment, including an opponent's talent and an athlete's perception of what it takes to win.

One of my clients is a world-class, professional tennis player. He serves in excess of 135 miles an hour, and he supplements that serve with exceptional basic, perceptual skills. If he could not change his game during a match, he would be okay but not exceptional.

Another client is a great baseball pitcher. By learning to modify his pitches during a game, he's progressed from being a good pitcher to a great pitcher who holds several season and post-season records, and he was recently voted into the Baseball Hall of Fame. I have witnessed him change his grip or his arm movement in the middle of a game to be more effective in that particular game.

A few years ago, a Major League Baseball (MLB) team with whom I worked signed a college player who was acknowledged to be one of the best hitters in the college ranks at that time. He had tremendous basic skills and a beautiful swing. When he reached the major-league level, he found that his basic swing was not good enough, but could not adjust it to hit against MLB pitchers. His explanation to our hitting coach was that his basic swing had been good enough through his high school and college years and he wasn't going to change it. His career was over less than a year after he was forced to become perceptual.

One reason why less than 2 percent of the players signed by professional teams make it to the major leagues is that they have great basic skills but are unable or unwilling to become perceptual in their performance. Other present and former high-profile athletes such as Pete Maravich, Michael Jordan, Kobe Bryant, and LeBron James, to name a few National Basketball Association (NBA) players, and Peyton Manning, Tom Brady, and Brett Favre in the National Football League (NFL) are examples of exceptionally perceptual athletes.

Too many times, a college education provides basic skills but doesn't help students progress to the perceptual level they need in a corporate environment. Therefore, when people start professional jobs, they expect to be successful because they have good basic skills.

It's a leader's job to help those people build on basic skills to reach a perceptual level. If leaders don't do that, then they're not doing a good job. There's nothing better for a leader than to have a team of players who have strong foundations and are willing to learn to use them to be perceptual. Obviously basic talent is a prerequisite to being successful, but equally obvious is that talent plus the ability to be perceptual takes you to another level.

A corporate environment offers daily opportunities for people to become perceptually active. As I mentioned, I've attended sales meetings where participants are encouraged and even directed to go back to their habits. This is troubling because it doesn't address how people can use their habits to become more perceptual in their performance. There's no doubt that people with solid habits perform at a relatively successful level and are usually very efficient. However, efficiency may not be the answer to long-term success.

In the past, a few companies stood above the rest simply because their products were the best. This has changed drastically. Like it or not, to stay in the marketplace, everybody in the company has to be good. The quality across companies is basically the same.

A critical question in the corporate world today is: If everyone has equal products, what separates us from the rest? The answer is simple. Efficiency is not good enough. You must also be effective. More companies are emphasizing the development of relationships. Customers are buying from people and companies they like and trust, those that can break from basic habits and help them solve problems. This changing dynamic makes it critical that corporate employees and management become more perceptual regarding co-workers and clients.

There are many universities that provide degrees in professional selling, corporate coaching, or life coaching. These I think are misleading degrees because they teach strong habits, but the students with the degrees have very few life skills.

Poor communication skills are the fertilizer for conflict. Good communication skills are the perceptual skills that breed winners. It also seems that corporate people who are perceptual are happier with themselves than those who depend on habits.

A great environment to distinguish between perceptual and habitual people is the airport, especially when there are flight delays. Habitual travelers are more likely to exhibit rage, attack the gate agent verbally, throw things, and use their cell phones to complain to friends who live thousands of miles away. So much wasted energy leads to an unhealthy lifestyle.

The perceptual travelers, however, will read a book, strike up a conversation with a stranger, take a quick nap, find a space where their children can move around and explore, or plug in the computer to get some work done or play a game.

Let's return to our parenting example because that is one undertaking that requires exceptional perception. As previously mentioned, parenting classes and books sell well but offer little practical knowledge. One reason they are popular is because parents are searching for answers to the challenges kids face in the educational environment. Many of these books present solutions to generic issues, which are unlike the ones people encounter in the real world. And the bottom line is that most people parent in the same way they were parented. We coach the way we were coached.

Today, however, kids are influenced more by peer groups than by parents. Decisions are more difficult to make, resulting in more difficult choices down the road. Parents have to be the most perceptual people in the world. It's a fine line to walk, instilling basic skills yet realizing that kids are going to be challenged daily. Consequently, parents must help their children to become more perceptual in their environment and behave accordingly, just like coaches and leaders do in sport and corporate situations. Parents must also remember that kids are going to make bad decisions that in the end enable them to learn how to recover more quickly and more effectively from adversity. Sometimes the most valuable learning experiences come from adverse situations. These situations are critical teaching tools for parents.

Other groups of people who encounter difficulties when they attempt to rely on habits are senior citizens and those with chronic illnesses. The environment may be a frustrating place for these people, primarily because they often are no longer able to execute their lifelong habits.

For example, I have multiple sclerosis (MS). MS is a very frustrating and devastating disease; the patient suicide rate is over seven times the national average. It's a disease for which there's no cure and it alters everything about how you go through life, even those things non-MS people never think about. Nothing meets the need to be perceptual more than having habits taken away. You have to be more aware of the surfaces on which you walk, of how you spend your energy, and of landmarks to help prevent you from getting lost. Multitasking is a thing of the past and planning ahead for events and vacations is very difficult. (I've always thought multitasking was a sign that a person was very average, pretty good at a lot of things, but not excellent at anything.) I've been living with MS for more than 12 years and am learning every day how to be more perceptive and creative to ensure that life is fun every day. There are too many symptoms to list here, but suffice it to say that for folks with chronic illnesses, it's is a daily challenge.

Age alone presents challenges to senior citizens. Now that I'm 72, I know that we cannot do many of the things we used to do. We must become more perceptive every day. Regardless of how many habits are taken away, the one trait that we all maintain control over is our attitude. There are no guarantees in life, but a positive attitude keeps the probability of success on your side.

Of particular importance in this area is that leaders understand that regardless of the task at hand, and in my case regardless of the medication I take, attitude is either your best friend or your worst enemy for the rest of your life. So it's critical that leaders who want to be up to date on the corporate techniques used in their environment still have a perception of the importance of the soft things in life, the intangibles—of which attitude may be the most important.

You know, in the context of the ideas presented in the previous chapters, it would seem that becoming perceptual is a natural consequence of lifelong learning experiences, but that's not true. The natural consequence is to be a very good habitual person. The critical challenge is to use this foundation to become a risk-taking person who accepts every situation and welcomes stress as an opportunity to increase his or her volume of perceptual growth.

What separates great race drivers from good drivers, great hitters from good hitters, great executives from good executives, great leaders from good leaders, head coaches from assistant coaches, happy people from sad people, productive people with chronic illness from sad people with chronic illness? The answer is that great, productive, happy people look forward to every day in order to flaunt their perceptual behaviors and to break away from habitual behaviors.

The more perceptual you become, the more successful you become in all areas of your life. As you become more equipped mentally, you recover more quickly from adversity. The more perceptual you become, the more you are able to recognize the same valuable qualities in other people. And the more perceptual you become, the more you recognize that the process of achieving goals must be fluid. The more perceptual you become, the more you learn how to surround yourself with people who support your emotional traits and help you massage habits. To become perceptual is an obvious challenge and will very often be uncomfortable, but the path to achieving success should include adversity.

When you become frustrated or anxious during certain situations, just remember that there are very few guarantees in life. One you can find in this chapter is that people with a solid foundation of talent who have learned how to use it in a perceptual way and who have positive expectations every day will always have a high probability of success. In real life, you cannot do everything you want. But by becoming more perceptual in your behavior, you can do more than you're doing today.

It's not a bad idea to list some of the basic habits that you've developed through education or life experiences, and then to take those habits and look very closely at each one to try to determine how it can be used in a perceptual way. It's a tough learning experience but very beneficial. And as a leader, if you can spot people on your team who have an overload of habits and just pick one habit to help them massage into perceptual behavior, then they will grow tremendously in a very short period of time. And as a leader, you'll grow as well because you become more aware of habits and how to change them.

Make no mistake, habits are a basic foundation. It's what I always tell people I work with: I don't care how good I make you feel mentally; if you can't play, you can't play. In other words, if you don't have talent, you can't play the game. And that talent is usually based on a good foundation of habits, but your productivity is based on how perceptive those habits become.

Final Thought

Help your team move from habitual to perceptual performance.

Habitual/Perceptual Behaviors

My Conditioned Habits

1. _____
2. _____
3. _____
4. _____
5. _____
6. _____
7. _____
8. _____
9. _____
10. _____

Perceptual Plan (Alternatives to Habits)

1. _____
2. _____
3. _____
4. _____
5. _____
6. _____
7. _____
8. _____
9. _____
10. _____

Leading Your Team from Habitual to Perceptual Behaviors

Chapter 9

Teach Your Team to Visualize

H ow important is visualization? If you're physically talented, have the knowledge to execute on the job, or have solid skills to perform, than why should you engage in mental practice? The answer is compelling. Match two people with equal physical talents in a competitive encounter, and the person who is stronger mentally will win most of the time.

Good leaders should learn to visualize, not only to enhance their own performance, but also to teach their team. It's a very important skill to have. It creates confidence and positive expectations.

In working with some of the best performers in the world for the last 45 years, I have found that the winners are not necessarily more talented than their competitors but they are much better prepared mentally. They are better organized, able to visualize, and able to recover quickly.

In the corporate environment, this has not been emphasized very much over the years, but I find it provides an incredible edge. For example, salespeople who visualize prior to a meeting will be better prepared than those who don't. If you're going to have a meeting with one of your team members, being able to visualize what will happen and anticipate different outcomes is a valuable tool to have.

Mental practice is an extremely valuable tool no matter the environment. It's used for two primary purposes. First, it enables you to review your competencies, in other words, to remember your assets. This motivates you and gives you a picture to guide you when executing. And that's the way that it's commonly used.

Second, mental practice is also useful as a learning tool. You can actually learn a skill, sales technique, or whatever. Basically, if you can see what you want to do in your mind and you have the assets to execute it, then you can mentally practice until you package the skill.

It seems incredible, but some people can learn to play sports before they ever try to do it physically. I know two individuals who have done this. One of them learned to play golf at a basic level before he ever picked up a club or teed up a ball. He did it by watching videotapes and then visualizing himself executing drives, putts, and other shots on the golf course. The other person became a fairly proficient tennis player simply by mentally practicing, visualizing himself playing the game. Using the techniques of mental practice, he learned the basic skills that enabled him to become a reasonably good tennis player in a very short period of time. Once he started to play, his proficiency accelerated remarkably because he had the basic skills firmly in his mind.

There is much more to mental practice than simply imagining yourself executing skills the correct way. This chapter will show you how to do it and what to avoid. Once you've looked at the mechanics of the whole process, then you will be equipped to take whatever you do and plug that activity into this basic model for mental practice. It will make you better professionally and personally. There is no question about that because it will make you more comfortable. It will reduce your anxiety level before you start and enable you to lower your post-performance anxiety level more quickly.

Research shows conclusively that mental practice is effective in performance enhancements. My colleagues and I, as early as the '60s and early '70s, conducted research with free throw shooting in basketball. We had four groups of basketball players who participated in the study. They were: one, a control group (no practice); two, a mental practice group; three, a physical practice group; and four, a mental and physical practice group. All four groups were equal when they started. Each group shot 25 free throws to start the seven-day study. The control group did no practice during the seven days. The mental practice group stood on the free throw line every day and mentally practiced 25 free throws, then walked away. The physical practice group came, shot 25 free throws, and left. The mental and physical group visualized taking 12 or 13 free throws and then finished up by physically taking 12 or 13. When the groups came back to be retested a week later, the no-practice group predictably had the worst results. The mental practice group scored significantly better than the no-practice group, indicating that at least at a basic level, skills were learned without actual physical participation. If you think it through, do it correctly, and have all the parts in place, you can actually learn the skill. The physical practice group, as expected, performed better than the mental practice group. Next, the mental and physical practice group went to the line. This group performed better than the other three groups. Similar results will be found for almost any motor skill that's researched over the years. It's a true indication of the value of mental practice.

If you receive and process information correctly, keep only the proper cues, package that together, and store it in your mind, you have the behaviors necessary to practice mentally whatever you have stored. However, if you store and mentally practice mistakes, then that's what you will execute.

The process often fails because of flaws in the mechanics of mental practice. One of those is speed of practice. It's critical that you mentally practice at the actual speed of whatever you intend to do. Obviously if you mentally practice at a faster speed, you set yourself up to execute physically in fast motion. If you visualize in slow motion, then you actually set your body up to respond in slow motion. It's a prerequisite to know how long it takes to execute a given skill so that you can mentally practice that skill in real time.

Teach Your Team to Visualize

In baseball, it's possible for me to tell if the pitcher is using true visualization. I ask him to step back, visualize the pitch, step up, and throw. Then he steps back off the mound, takes a quick breath, steps up, and throws and says, "I saw it." He claims to have visualized the correct pitch, despite taking only one second to visualize what should take several seconds. My reply: "You must have seen it faster than I could." If, in fact, he completed the mental exercise in one second, he set himself up to fail simply because he's going to overthrow or speed up his motion, and it's not going to be natural. It's so imperative that you visualize in real time.

One of the most significant impacts of mental practice is an attitudinal change. Positive anticipation of an event provides at least an opportunity for success. People can foresee the consequences of their actions if they walk through the visualization process and antici-pate the consequences. This ability to prepare is another critical factor in performance.

In order for visualization to help you, it's absolutely essential that you know what your capabilities are. Review your assets and liabilities. You must understand what your entry behaviors are and you need to visualize those, but be careful not to go overboard. It's not only frustrating, but also discouraging to visualize things that you're not capable of executing. For example, I can visualize myself throwing a 95-mile-an-hour fastball at the stadium, but when they put the speed gun on me, my top speed is only about 42. So you need to visualize what you're capable of doing. The old cliché *if you can see it, you can do it* is absolutely a lie. If you visualize what you're not capable of doing, then you become frustrated when your execution falls short.

You always need to stretch your system and push your abilities, but you should visualize realistic skills that you're capable of executing given your talents, your tools, and your mechanics. What you visualize is something you may not have done before but are capable of doing, reaching a higher level of performance within your capabilities. It's a commonsense approach to execution.

A pitcher who is able to step back from the mound, take a deep breath, visualize the next pitch—which takes about three seconds—then step up and throw that pitch has more confidence and motivation. Visualization becomes an incentive to perform better, and many times it will yield more consistent results.

If you make a speech, for example, then review it afterwards and visualize your punch line that fell flat, then the next time you try to avoid that mistake, the probability is high that you'll repeat it until you correct it mentally. You want to avoid visualizing the bad joke because replaying it in your mind sets you up for an incorrect performance.

Look to previous experiences only to make mental corrections. No matter what your environment, don't dwell on past negative experiences. Adjust the visualization and go to the next action. Never perform the previous execution without making necessary changes. In other words, don't perform off mistakes. As I've said before: Never leave anything bad unless you're going toward something good. That's true in physical performance, true in the corporate environment, and true for your mental practice.

Hitters visualize a swing. They step up to the batter's box and imagine themselves swinging and hitting the ball. They step into the batter's box and try to execute to that visualization. Golfers do the same thing. If a golfer wants the avoid carrying mental baggage after a bad shot, she steps back, visualizes a good shot, steps up, and executes according to what she replayed in her mind. There's another way this works, too. If the golfer hits a great shot, she can step back, visualize it, and store it mentally for later use, even if she doesn't manage to catch it on video to watch an actual replay. A mental replay provides her with the same positive information.

If you have a great sales meeting, then immediately after it's over, you need to find time to be alone and visualize what just took place in

Teach Your Team to Visualize

the meeting. In this way, you can store that data and execute the same way in the future. Don't visualize and think about the things that went wrong. Visualize and execute mentally the things that were correct. You'll build a mental data package to draw on at the next meeting.

Leaders are in a unique position to help their team execute visualization. As a leader, you remind your team every day to mentally replay good experiences because those are the things that you want to store for future use.

Parents can visualize conversations they're going to have with teachers, or with their children, or with each other. By doing this they're able to anticipate questions, conflicts, and the consequences of their actions, which can be very effective. Teachers should use visualization as a daily process before classes. In fact, the execution of any activity will benefit from the visualization process.

One of the top international tennis coaches, Dennis Van der Meer, once defined true visualization at a tennis clinic: "True visualization is when you can see it in color." A pro golfer recently made the same comment. The idea is that in true visualization you can see everything. You can see your clothes. You can see the course. You can see everything that's going on around you. That gives you a vivid picture of what you want to do and how you want to do it. The whole visualization process means that you mentally see your performance from beginning to end. You don't just see the end result.

If you ask golfers if they visualize, 90 percent will say yes; and when you ask them what they visualize, 90 percent of that group will probably tell you they see the ball going where they want it to go. True visualization is reviewing the process.

Again, as we previously discussed, your emphasis needs to be on the process, and the best way to keep your focus is to visualize it. If you set out to visualize a sales meeting, but you only visualize signing the deal, you have no mental preparation for what will get you to that point. Similarly, a golfer who only visualizes the ball sinking into the hole would have no mental storage about what caused the ball to get there. True visualization is again seeing everything from start to finish—don't ever leave out anything. With the whole sequence in mind, you can make corrections in your performance or make adjustments in how you are communicating with people.

In these effective mental practice sessions, you get to the point where, if you want to make a change in whatever it is that you're executing, you can plug in the change you want to make and then continue to visualize. You can make changes in performance through visualization before you ever execute. That's a benefit for visualizing very specific correct things. To do this correctly, you may need to describe the activity and create a specific list of segmented events making up the total package.

Visualization is most effective if you have yourself videotaped. Everyone needs a videotape of his or her performance, if possible. As an aid to my own speaking, I have videotapes of past speeches and seminars. When I work with golfers, I videotape every swing, including drives, long irons, short irons, sand shots, approach shots, fringe shots, and putts. My objective is to provide the golfer with a videotape of what he or she is able to execute. I do it with every sport—videotapes are used extensively with football and baseball players. The videotape gives them a ready-made picture that they can pull up at any time. If possible, get a videotape of your performance and review it a number of times. It's not uncommon for me to repeat a certain pitch 10 to 15 times back to back so I can bombard the pitcher's system with what he's able to execute. Then it's easier for him to mentally pull out that picture and throw that great pitch. This holds true in other situations, as well.

It's critical to note here that you only view positive recordings. Don't view videos of mistakes. If you are working in a corporate job, don't review tapes of mistakes you've made in meetings or in one-on-one sessions. Always record correct execution because that's where you want to go. On the one hand, if you videotape mistakes, then you

Teach Your Team to Visualize

tend to go into a meeting trying to *not* make mistakes. On the other hand, if you videotape positive performance, you go into a meeting with the intent to execute positive performance.

Salespeople consistently improve their presentations by videotaping them and playing them back as described. These people have more energy because they are not consumed by all the things that could go wrong. They are also more successful more often. Use of video footage can be a critical factor in visualization.

When approaching this technique as a mechanical process, there are seven critical elements:

1. Always see yourself executing correctly.

2. Always mentally see correct techniques.

3. See everything involved in every part from start to finish—and see it in color—every time you repeat it.

4. Visualize the action at actual speed. If you omit parts or you can't visualize clearly certain parts, then go back and start over. Don't ever muddle your way through and store incorrect material.

   I experienced a good example of the actual speed process firsthand when I worked with a world-class ice-skater. She was ranked 150 in the world. Now, in a routine that's two minutes long, you have to be sharp; you have to be quick in all your movements. I noticed when I watched her that her jumps were slow. She was slow getting into the correct position. So I asked her to visualize the routine from start to finish, which should take two minutes. Her visualization took six minutes. That explained to me why she was slow in execution. So I had her work with her coach at least three times a week to sit down and visualize her performance until she was able to visualize it in two minutes. Once she got to that point and she could do it whenever she wanted within two minutes, her world ranking went from 150 to

50, and we did nothing with mechanics. It was simply because we worked on her mental preparation.

5. Remember you're trying to develop total confidence and mental consistency. That's your goal in visualization.

6. Repeat the mental practice several times during each session. Do not mentally practice one time and execute. Mentally practice several times and don't rush, but do it in real time. This deliberate visualization will enable you to set yourself up so that you're motivated and you have an incentive to execute. At that point, you almost get anxious to execute because you've just visualized a correct performance.

7. When you reach the place where you're going to execute your skills, visualize everything just before performance.

Once the mental process becomes conditioned, you won't necessarily have to do it every time, but you need to pick your times to do it. It's comforting to know that if you have it in your mind, you can execute it.

If you need to make changes in whatever you're performing, then you need only to pull the mental picture into the conscious mind and plug in the execution and do it again and again. Repeat the initial process until the change becomes part of the conditioned response when you're making corrections.

Remember that the prerequisite to the success of mental practice is that you know how to execute correctly and know what you can do. This means that, number one, you don't think you can do it, you don't wonder if you can do it, you *know* you can do it; number two, you visualize only correct skills. This is critical. If you mentally practice mistakes, as previously mentioned, you're going to make mistakes. To compound this problem, if you visualize mistakes and then you try to not make mistakes, anything you do wrong will be worse than it would have been otherwise.

Any time you feel like you're losing concentration or rhythm or focus, then you use the visualization process. You can enhance your concentration by using a key word or phrase as a trigger. Imagine a football place kicker who tells himself to be aggressive, make good contact, and have good leg speed. If you visualize a conversation, then you walk in and you're ready to start the conversation. You might say something to yourself such as "go for it" or "let it go" or something that's significant to you. Choose a word or phrase that pulls everything you visualize back to the front of your mind so you're able to execute. The trigger is a critical part to the performance. It actually brings your mental practice to physical realization.

In sport, especially in golf and hitting in baseball, your visualization or your trigger word needs to take you to the ball, not be a distraction that takes you away from the ball. If, for example, your last thought is stay back, then you're going to stay back and you're going to be late on pitches. In golf, if your last thought is good back swing, then you may or may not hit a good shot.

In place kicking, if you visualize a field goal, you need to make sure your visualization draws you into the behavior you are trying to execute. If a place kicker doesn't visualize, he runs a risk of making two mistakes. First, if he tries too hard to make it, 80 percent of the time he pulls it and is too far left. If he tries too hard to not miss it, then he pushes it and misses it to the right. He can only be successful when he lets himself kick.

In meetings, you can only be successful if you visualize letting yourself perform in whatever environment you are likely to experience. It could be one-on-one communication or it could be in a conference environment. Always *let your talent take you toward you goal*. That's a very important phrase you need to remember. In other words, execute the process well and let it happen. Don't try to force it to happen.

I work with a pitcher on a National League baseball team who gets caught up in the moment, so I put a white L on his glove so that when begins to wind up, he'll see it. The L means *let yourself pitch*. Sometimes when he was getting too emotional, he'd see the L, step back, take a deep breath, and tell himself to let himself pitch.

There are any number of things you can do to help yourself use triggers and initiate the process, and I've included an example here that you can adapt to any environment. I use golf because it is an easy process to look at, but you can adapt it to any environment that you're in.

When you review this chapter, it becomes very obvious that this is commonsense information. If there is anything you can do to make yourself better as a leader or as a member of a team, then you need to learn how and do it every single day. Visualization is one of those things. Why leave things to chance when you can visualize and anticipate and set yourself up to be successful? You find that a lot of ex-athletes working in the corporate environment use visualization because they did it in sport. That doesn't mean it's only appropriate for athletes; it's appropriate for everybody.

Final Thought

Always visualize correct performance.

Visualization

Example of Visualization Using Golf

Before trying to visualize, break down the parts of your swing, starting with club selection and ending with the follow-through. Then place that shot breakdown into the total sequence outlined below.

1. Select club
2. Visualize
   a. Address
   b. Take-away
   c. Backswing
   d. Swing
   e. Contact
   f. Follow-through
   g. See the ball's flight
3. Physically address the ball
4. Use trigger
5. Execute shot
6. Mentally store good shots

List the steps to visualize team meetings and/or individual meetings.

1. _____

2. _____

3. _____

4. _____

5. _____

6. _____

7. _____

8. _____

9. _____

10. _____

11. _____

12. _____

13. _____

14. _____

15. _____

Teach Your Team to Visualize

Chapter 10

Motivate the Environment, Not the Team

As a leader, you must recognize the value of motivation. More important than the type of motivation that's used, timing is probably the most important aspect. When given at an inappropriate time, motivation is no more valuable than no encouragement at all. In fact, it may be more harmful to performance. In both the sport and corporate environments, I've always thought overcoaching is worse than no coaching at all.

Leaders shouldn't feel the need to coach people every day. That won't make you look more like a leader. True leaders understand when motivation is needed, when it's not, and when to let people do their jobs but be available if they need reinforcement.

Poorly timed efforts have an artificial air about them. To be effective, motivation must occur when the person will most benefit from a feeling of recognition, belonging, or success. It doesn't have to be some reward system that's involved.

As I've noted in other chapters, many times the activity itself will motivate a person. In sports, golf is a good example. Some people participate in golf not to compete but because the sport presents a challenge, every shot is different. One good shot will motivate players to continue to play. You often hear at golf courses that if you hit one great shot in a round, which may consist of 90 to 100 shots, that one shot will bring you back to play the game again.

The same can hold true in a corporate environment. You can have a pretty tough day but one accomplishment can give you the incentive to come back and crank it up again the next day. You need to be able to transfer that attitude to your daily environment personally as well as professionally so that if several things don't go well, that one thing that does will be enough of an incentive to get you motivated for the next day. We need to recognize the little things as they come to us.

There are several different ways to motivate people. First and foremost, you are trying to instill the desire to explore complexity, which is closely linked to motivation. For example, when engaged in a highly competitive, complex skill, it's probably better to be moderately motivated because of all the information you have to process. In other words, it's best to not be emotionally over the edge while performing something that's really complex.

However, when performing a relatively simple skill that may be part of what you do every day of your corporate career, a higher level of motivation is appropriate because there's much less information to process. Also, the type of motivation is important in regard to what it is meant to do, whether it's *intrinsic* or *extrinsic*. To clarify, *intrinsic motivation* is satisfaction that comes from doing a good job and being fulfilled by the work itself. This can only come from within a person and is very hard to foster in a negative environment. *Extrinsic motivation*, on the other hand, comes from material gain. In the context of a job, it means that people don't find the work to be fulfilling; instead, they see the job as necessary activity that provides them money, status, or other material benefits. People who are extrinsically motivated are going to stay with your team only until a better offer comes along—whether that means a bigger paycheck or fancier title— because they're not motivated by the work, the company, or the environment. If these aspects of a job are not fulfilling, a person can find motivation only through material things. It's much more beneficial to you as a leader to work with people who are intrinsically motivated, people who are motivated by the fulfillment they get from doing the job, by being around your team, by verbal reinforcement, by recognition, and by fulfilling expectations that you have passed onto them.

There are probably times when we use both types of motivation, but for long-term results I don't think there's any question that intrinsic motivation is much more valuable for long-term impact. And the timing is obviously important.

It's akin to the critical learning periods children go through. These times, which we often call *teachable moments*, are when children reach a certain level emotionally, socially, and physically. That's when the package comes together, so to speak, making it an appropriate time for them to learn certain kinds of skills. I think in adulthood there are still critical periods where motivation is either going to be appropriate or inappropriate based on where a person is psychologically at the time.

In youth sports, it's very interesting that many times we judge kids based on their physical appearance. Some kids are big and strong, and we think they're prepared to enter competition, so we don't realize that their size may be very misleading. They may be physically developed, but at the same time they may not be socially and emotionally prepared for competition.

Motivation should never come across as being insincere or superficial either. It should always be exercised at a time when it can be accepted as an honest effort to help a person improve and to accomplish things that they haven't done recently. This is especially true for people with chronic illnesses. It's important that if you're going to be motivated to do something, you recognize the clutter your mind. In other words, understand the things that are taking up your mental space and don't get caught up in being motivated to remove everything at one time.

The same thing holds true in the corporate environment. Too many people have too many things on their mind at the same time, and they become what we call *multitaskers*. As I mentioned in the previous chapter, I've never had much respect for multitaskers because I think

Motivate the Environment, Not the Team

they're usually good at a lot of things but not really great at anything. To avoid falling into a trap of multitasking but not actually getting much done, it's necessary to prioritize the things cluttering your to-do list. Then, you have an incentive to either work on it, store it away for later, or to learn to live with it.

You can't look at the whole package at one time. You have to take each factor that's perceived as clutter, deal with it individually, and set up an action so that you're motivated to accomplish something specific. This makes it possible to evaluate your progress at the end of the day.

Motivation really stirs your system. It is a psychological phenomenon that has a physiological impact. In other words, you get emotional, you get anxious, and once your emotions reach a certain level, then you're motivated to accomplish some task.

It's interesting that motivation is one of the most frequently discussed concepts in a corporate environment but it is probably the most misunderstood. After 45 years of working with athletes, the first question I get asked in meetings is, "How do you motivate athletes?" My response has always been that I've never attempted to motivate anyone. I think intrinsic motivation is the route to go. Extrinsic motivation is superficial and short lived.

Motivation is really just a way of arousing your system. We've talked about the mechanics of motivation and the types of motivation, but in real life motivation means you're trying to accomplish something every day. In other words, if you get up in the morning and you've written down some goals for the day, then those goals will provide you with the incentive to accomplish something. People are either motivated to accomplish something or they're motivated to not fail. I have very little patience with that second group. In the corporate environment, they're great survivors, but they're not going to help the team win. Their attitude also seems to be contagious and eventually everybody will fall into the trap of trying to not fail, and the team never progresses.

It's critical for a leader in the corporate environment to understand when people are trying to not fail—and it's very obvious in most cases. There are only two ways to proceed when you encounter someone who is trying not to fail. You can try to help them change their outlook and find some intrinsic motivation, or you can have them leave the environment. I think that most people who are trying to not fail are pretty scary to be around and they live their lives in a very superficial way. We all need to be motivated to accomplish something every single day.

In other words, there are no guarantees in life, but if you're motivated to try to clear out the mental clutter and get something done, then at least the probability is on your side that you're going to accomplish that. Those things don't really happen by accident, and so you have to have directed energy and emotion in order to accomplish something. We call it *selective attention*.

Think for a moment of the powerful environment provided by support meetings for any number of negative situations people find themselves in. One of the problems I have with support meetings is that many times they are filled with other people who feel terrible and want everybody to know how bad they feel. That being the case, people who go into those meetings feeling pretty good can leave the meeting feeling pretty bad because nothing positive happened. Negativity is contagious, but a lack of positivity can also have a bad effect. My suggestion to folks who attend support meetings is that if you don't leave a meeting with something in hand that will give you a chance to do more tomorrow, then you're in the wrong meeting.

The same thing can happen in departments or teams in a corporate environment. If you have an office group of five people who are happy and motivated and then one negative person with the motivation to merely survive comes into the office, it won't take long before that one person drags down the whole office attitude.

People who are motivated to accomplish something in life are risk takers. They're willing to fail, but they're also able to recover quickly.

Motivate the Environment, Not the Team

People who are motivated to not fail accomplish very little in their lives, and so it's very important that you understand the difference between extrinsic and intrinsic motivation. The people who are usually going to be the negative, unmotivated people are usually motivated only by extrinsic rewards.

As a leader, you need to understand the difference in people's needs and drives, and the other mechanics of motivation, so that you can develop a plan to move ahead in your life.

As a multiple sclerosis (MS) patient, there are times when I might be motivated to walk a mile. There are no guarantees, but at least I feel there some incentive to try. If I don't make it all the way, at least I've put in the effort and I can feel good about that, especially if I can go farther tomorrow than I did today. But without motivation or a sense of fulfillment, belonging, or self-esteem, I'm not going to accomplish very much.

Motivation forms the foundation we need to accomplish goals and live life in a very fulfilling way. Without motivation, without incentive, without writing things down, without having specific goals, there's very little probability that you're ever going to accomplish what you're capable of doing because your motivation is going to be disorganized and untargeted. You need to be directed so that your energy is used in a very productive and positive manner.

Now, let's talk a bit about *selective attention*. Motivation can be a tremendous waste of energy or a tremendous asset, depending on whether or not you have selective attention. In other words, if your energy is targeted to accomplish something, you are far more likely to succeed than if you fully dedicate your efforts to avoid failure. If you take four-year-old kids out and teach them how to throw a ball, they initially will fatigue very early. Why? Because they're paying attention to too many cues in the environment, such as other kids, trees, birds, cars, whatever might be there. But as you take them into that environment more and more, they will be less distracted by the noise, so they will be able to focus on the cues they need for catching and throwing the ball. Once they do that, they can throw and catch all day because they learn to use their energy in the right places.

Leaders in the corporate environment need to understand the needs and the drives of the people around them. They need to know that they're pushing the right buttons. It's not enough to simply coach in the way we were coached. It's interesting to note that if you list the things that motivate you and you have your team members list the things that motivate them, there might not be the alignment you expect. You will find that you are trying to motivate other people in the way you like to be motivated, and it's a failing process. Motivation takes time and energy, but unless you are able to tailor your approach to the people you work with, there's nothing positive to be realized from it.

So it's critical that, as a leader, you understand how and when to offer motivation, and maybe even more important, whether you try to motivate people at all.

I've always felt that if you create a motivating environment that people want to be a part of (Chapter 7), you'll be able to spark intrinsic motivation in your team. That will help you keep your people longer, keep them happier, and keep them more productive.

Final Thought

Don't motivate people, rather create a motivating environment.

 **Intrinsic/Extrinsic Motivators**

Intrinsic Motivators for You as a Leader

1. _____

2. _____

3. _____

4. _____

5. _____

6. _____

7. _____

8. _____

9. _____

10. _____

11. _____

12. _____

13. _____

14. _____

15. _____

Extrinsic Motivators for You as a Leader

1. _____
2. _____
3. _____
4. _____
5. _____
6. _____
7. _____
8. _____
9. _____
10. _____
11. _____
12. _____
13. _____
14. _____
15. _____

Intrinsic Motivators for Your Team Members

1. _____
2. _____
3. _____
4. _____
5. _____
6. _____
7. _____
8. _____
9. _____
10. _____
11. _____
12. _____
13. _____
14. _____
15. _____

Extrinsic Motivators for Your Team Members

1. _____
2. _____
3. _____
4. _____
5. _____
6. _____
7. _____
8. _____
9. _____
10. _____
11. _____
12. _____
13. _____
14. _____
15. _____

Motivate the Environment, Not the Team

Chapter 11

Lead by Thriving on Stress

L earn how to thrive on stress. Stress provides a tremendous incentive to perform well. Leaders should spend less time reading about it and going to stress-management seminars, which bombard you with information about stress's harmful effects, and more time making it an asset.

Stress is unquestionably a determining factor in success versus survival. It comes into play in everything you do every day, both professionally and personally.

On the one hand, leaders thrive on stress. I've never met a good leader who was not a stress seeker. Survivors, on the other hand expend enormous amounts of energy avoiding stressors. Consequently, they only survive at best.

Whether they're working in a sport or corporate environment or working through a chronic illness, the people I have worked with over the past 45 years realize that stress is always there. Initially, it is perceived as a negative by almost everyone. But we need to understand that stress levels do not make us sick or cause other negative things in our lives. Rather, it is how we perceive and react to stress that can have an unhealthy effect. This will be surprising to you if you've always been told that stress is a negative, even overwhelming influence in your life.

How much time do you spend every day trying to rid your life of stress? How much does stress cost industry every year? Billions of dollars are spent by corporations to deal with stress. Much of that cost takes the form of disability payments. Employees can retire from some professions after seven years with as much as 75 percent disability because of job-related stress.

It would seem that stress is a significantly negative factor in terms of productivity and health. However, probably more than 80 percent of stress factors are neither positive nor negative when they confront your system. They become negative primarily because of how people perceive them. We hear the word *stress* and immediately begin thinking of all the things that are wrong with our lives. We seldom think of the positive aspects that actually act as motivators to make positive changes that will benefit us. Stress management seminars are very popular ways to teach people how to relax and eliminate stress, but too often these seminars are nothing more than knee-jerk reactions to a traditional definition of stress. The truth is that your mindset causes most stressors to become more negative.

Of course, I'm referring mostly to those stressors that cause you mental anguish. There are physical stressors that are obviously extremely negative, at least initially, to those who suffer from disabilities, have had accidents, or have chronic illnesses. Even in those instances, there are enough assets present within your system so that, if you use the stressors as motivators to accomplish things, your life can continue to be very productive.

By definition, stress is the amount of wear and tear the body and mind experiences. It has a physiological impact on the body. For instance, stress when you walk puts pressure on the joints in your legs. When you throw, you put stress on your arms and shoulders. When you talk, there's stress on your vocal cords. Even when you breathe, there's stress on your respiratory system. Another physiological example is the fight-or-flight response that is triggered by major emotional stressors.

So there are physical stressors and responses everywhere every day in everyone's life. You need to accept that this is true and will probably always be. When you fail to accept these physical and psychological stressors as normal, they can develop into major issues.

There are many ways to deal with stress, but the first thing we have to realize is that stressors are not necessarily meant to shut your system down. In fact, most of the time, they are meant to be incentives to enable you to become better. Stressors make you what you are and drive you to where you need to be. They can bring you to the emotional edge and get you where you need to be in order to obtain that optimal level of performance. If they don't drive you to become better, stressors may make you worse through illness such as depression or burnout.

Success or failure depends on your perception of these stressors. The operative term is *perception*. Because of both personal and professional conditioning, people tend to panic when under great stress. They let stress control their lives. This is an issue for anyone at any age. I've known parents whose five-year-old kindergartners were in counseling due to stress in their environment. I've known people no older than 26 who have had heart attacks related to stress.

Stress really does not discriminate. In the workplace, stress-related problems cause widespread symptoms such as headaches, nervous tension, irritability, burnout, wasted time, and poor time management. All contribute in some respects to absenteeism, which has been a major issue in business, especially in the present economic environment.

To repeat, up to 80 percent of stress is neither positive nor negative. Traffic is an obvious example of a stressor that isn't inherently negative. Others common stressors are deadlines, shortages of financial resources, and other constraints that propose difficulty. But anything can be a stressor, including other people, children, and, of course, bills. Almost everything you can imagine that affects your life creates some degree of stress. All these stressors can be assets to your productivity if you see them as incentives to success; otherwise they can become detrimental. The key is how you deal with them. This is a serious and conscious choice that every person has to make. By choosing to

Lead by Thriving on Stress

perceive those stressors, if at all possible, as bringing potential positives to your life, you can harness their power and thrive.

At one point in my life, I was partially paralyzed. I was in the Mayo Clinic in Rochester, Minnesota, and was diagnosed with a stress-related condition for which I had to be hospitalized. Though I've never been sure if stress was really the problem, I nonetheless recovered and began to do about 10 times as much as I had done before. My productivity soared because I learned to take better care of myself. I exercised more and I ate better. I looked at things from a different perspective. Since then, I've never been happier personally or professionally, despite the many stressors I have encountered.

In 2004 I was diagnosed with multiple sclerosis (MS). People with chronic illness understand that stress is a major issue for patients, and I was definitely under pressure. I had no idea what MS was, and I had no idea how devastating it could be. The only thing I knew was that it was not good.

After spending many days and nights wondering and worrying about what was going to happen and feeling sorry for myself, I came to realize that there was a purpose to all of this. I acknowledged that MS was indeed a stressor, but I could use it to become a better person. I had probably gotten complacent in my profession. I believe my programs were still good, but I'm not sure that I appreciated them as much as I should have. I began to work harder. I found I had more control over my time and became, I think, more productive than before I was diagnosed. I certainly learned to appreciate every day of my life more than I had before.

With that in mind, I made a conscious choice to turn the stress of my MS diagnosis into a positive incentive in my life, and I never looked back. Obviously not everyone is able to do that, but at least we all have the emotional capability to take control of our lives under stress and salvage more good things to make ourselves better and to be happy.

As a leader in a corporate setting, it's critical that you understand that stress is a part of any environment. It's your responsibility as a leader to help your team members evaluate the stress, categorize it, analyze it, and use it as an incentive. If people don't react to stress in a positive way, then the end result is exhaustion of the system, and obviously no one wants that. But it's your first responsibility, not only as a leader but also as a corporate person, to demonstrate how you deal with stress in a positive way so that your team can pick up on it.

There are many typical reactions to stress and we will discuss four or five of those. There are just as many ways to recognize stress and deal with it in a positive way, and we will also discuss doing that. The important note here is that when you have many things on your mind that you're thinking about, worrying about, or trying to attend to, you're going to have undue stress in your life. You may try to give everything equal consideration and time, and hope for positive results, but that's not going to help you succeed. You have to begin to prioritize. You can't be happy as a multitasker. As I like to describe it, multitasking *puts mud in the water*. It clouds your judgment and your ability to dedicate your full efforts to the most important tasks at hand. You have to be able to prioritize several stressors before you can make them incentives, so you must be able to focus on two or three things instead of trying to tackle everything at once. We've talked about this in several chapters. You need to be able to sit down and list all the things that are on your mind, prioritize, and eliminate. You'll need to give your emotional attention to those items that are most important at this particular time.

Consider for a moment a person who is physically disabled. She is still the same person she has always been, but she has a new stressor and will have to figure out new ways to do the same things she has always done. It is possible. It is a choice that is critical to make.

If you have a chronic illness or memory issues, as in my case, you may have to write more things down. Despite these change, you have to learn to enjoy every single day. Instead of setting an extensive,

Lead by Thriving on Stress

long-term goal, set smaller daily or hourly goals. That will help you deal with stress. Go back and review Chapter 4 and you'll find that setting goals in the suggested manner will indeed be an asset to you.

If you have something specific that you're trying to do, as opposed to letting the stress in your life cause you to put things off or to procrastinate, set goals to help you get the job done. You'll feel better having accomplished some things on your list, even if they are small. As I've said before, it's easy to feel bad and hard to feel good, but once you do the things that are necessary to feel good, like using stress as an incentive, it's amazing how much more productive you can be.

There are a lot of stress reactions. They are generally categorized into five different areas. I don't think any of these five are particularly helpful to you, but they're typical ways that people deal with stress, and you need to know about them. The first is *withdrawal*. In other words people remove themselves from a stressful environment. Sometimes I think strategic withdrawal is okay if you need to get your ideas together and think about things before you confront the stressor. But just withdrawing in order to avoid emotional exposure to stress can be detrimental to your system because, when you come back to the environment, most likely the stress will still be there and it will probably be even more significant than before. It's very important for leaders to notice when people withdraw and understand why it happens. Then they can take advantage of a teachable moment to help people confront their stressors head on.

The second response to stress is helplessness. I think everyone at some point has experienced this feeling, especially when you're sitting in traffic, having a bad day, or feeling ill and medication doesn't seem to be helping. A feeling of helplessness can creep into your system very quickly. It inhibits recovery and can shut your system down, so you need to do whatever you can to avoid it. If you begin to feel helpless in a stressful environment, then try to think of some situations you've been in that caused similar feelings and think about what you did to recover. Doing so will give you a springboard for recovery.

Internalizing is the third way many people attempt to cope with stress. A person who internalizes stress does not talk about it, deal with it, or let other people on the team step in and help. I think this may be the most harmful to your body and the most hazardous to your health because the more you hold stress in, the more apt you are to have problems with headaches, ulcers, rashes, and other kinds of physical manifestations of internalized stress. Internalizing is a very scary way to deal with stress. A difficult situation doesn't get any better by holding it inside.

The fourth approach to dealing with stress is overcontrol. This is of particular importance to people who want to be leaders. Many times when things seem to be out of control and going in a negative direction, tightening your grip seems to be the most logical step to take. This is often not true. Many people in stressful environments attempt to over-control what's happening around them. In a corporate environment, these people tend to become micromanagers, and subsequently they have a negative impact on the office environment and lose a lot of good employees.

I can recall at least one situation in sports where the general manager was an incredibly overcontrolling person. Because of that, the team was not permitted to do their job without answering to him first. My feeling has always been that if you hire well, it's best to let your people work. In sports, the manager's job is to have good players, put them on the field, and let them play. Overmanaging is worse than not managing at all.

If you have good people on your team, an environment with less control is better than one where the manager is domineering. No one can improve without the opportunity to take ownership over their work. Overcontrol, especially for the long term, is not a viable way to deal with stress. In rare case, brief periods of overmanaging may be

Lead by Thriving on Stress

beneficial to get people back on track, but once they are there it's your responsibility as a leader to help them understand that they have a job to do, a good environment in which to work, and a leader who is going to let them play the game.

Emotional outbursts are the fifth way people unsuccessfully cope with stress. This is my favorite because it is the most interesting. Many people who seem to be pretty mild mannered, quiet people can all of a sudden become overwhelmed by stress that they have been internalizing. When it gets to be too much for their system, they have an emotional outburst. Everyone has probably experienced this at one time or another, either in front of other people or when alone. But an emotional outburst of 30 seconds may cost you years of loyalty and respect from the people around you. It may even have cost you friendships.

I've always thought that getting mad is not an issue, in sports or in the corporate environment. My perception is that if you don't get mad, you don't care. The reality is that anger enables us to have a catharsis for our emotions, but it's critical that you get past those feelings very quickly. When I talk about speed of recovery from adversity, I mean that it's okay to get upset, but you need to get over it in a reasonable amount of time. You see it in sports and in the corporate environment.

If your emotional outburst causes you to lose the respect of your people, you're basically lost as a leader. The only way you can regain respect is to go to a new environment because most of the people who witnessed your outburst are going to be suspicious of your motives for being nice to them. So once you lose respect, you're done.

If you look at these five ways of dealing with stress, I think you would be hard pressed to convince me that any of them is desirable. You need to give a lot of thought to how you want to react to stress, at least emotionally.

If you look at how people typically try to relieve stress, one good example is running. Many people consider running to be a good way to relieve emotional stress, but it puts tremendous physical stress on your knees, hips, and joints. Running is not always a relief to stress, and many times it causes more stress. Other people will play golf or play tennis for stress relief, but if you've ever played, you understand very quickly that the sport environment often causes more stress than it relieves. So unless you play for the right reasons, then you probably shouldn't consider it a way to relieve stress.

Going beyond those five negative ways of dealing with stress, I would like to put forth a positive method: look forward to and thrive on stress. Stress will either make you great or end your life; it's your choice to make. If you ask 100 people who are recovering from heart attacks brought on by stress how they feel, an overwhelming number will tell you they feel better than they've felt in 20 years and they're more productive. My question to you is very simple: Do you have to have a heart attack before you get healthy?

After dealing with professional athletes, corporations, and many folks with chronic illness, I've developed a few keys for thriving on stress. These keys may at least give you an idea of how to pursue positive outcomes. Remember that all the stressors can be either potential assets or liabilities. It's your choice to make. In fact, the most dangerous stressors seem to be the small, nagging things that come up every day, not necessarily major life events.

I think a lot of people who have gone through catastrophic injuries and life-altering situations have gotten through them and are stronger than they were, at least emotionally. It's the little things that pop up every day that you probably need to learn how to react to. It's the responsibility of leaders to help their teammates deal with these niggling little stressors on a daily basis.

The first key to thriving in stressful situations is to separate the stressors from the symptoms. We often react with pretty significant emotion to symptoms, but we never get to the sources. If you recall our discussion of assets and liabilities (Chapter 2), I said that on a list of

155

10 liabilities, you will find that there may be 2 or 3 true liabilities and the other 7 or 8 items are really just symptoms of those. The same thing happens when you examine your stressors. If you write down all the things that cause stress in your life—there could be 10 or 20 or 50 things—when you review them, you will likely find that you are dealing with only 4 or 5 real stressors. The rest of the things are symptoms of those basic issues. Realizing this will enable you to get off to a much more positive start in dealing with stress.

Another thing that is critical to managing stress is the ability to drain your emotions from negative situations. The better you can neutralize emotions during conflicts, the better off you're going to be. One way to do that is to list the elements of a particular stressor and then, when emotions begin to run higher than is comfortable, look back at what you wrote to regain your balance. If you're going to have a meeting or other situation that you expect to be stressful, beforehand list the things that you want to address. Then, if the conversation becomes emotional, you can always review what you wrote. This prevents an emotional discussion of stressors, which makes stress worse.

I had a corporate client recently who was dealing with a very tough situation, and he was basically intimidated by the person he was dealing with. I suggested that before the next meeting he list the topics that he wanted to discuss, keeping it as objective as possible. Then, when he started to feel emotional during the meeting, he could go use the list to stay focused and neutralize his feelings. That conversation went well, the outcome was good, and now the two have a decent working relationship.

The third key to using stress to your advantage is to take some time to make a comprehensive list of all your personal and professional stressors. Don't worry about presenting them in any particular order; just write each one down as you think of it. After that, you will be able to identify a lot of things that you can turn into incentives. For example, there are a lot of stressors in relationships that we need to deal with in order to make them stronger. As we mentioned before, withdrawing can make a situation worse, and it can get to the point where there's no recovery. If you block communication in a relationship for long, then the reestablishment of communication becomes very awkward and uncomfortable. If you are aware of your stressors and share this knowledge with others, you will be able to manage your emotions and build stronger relationships.

Once you have your list of stressors, decide which can be changed to become assets. The key to channeling stress so it helps you thrive is tying it to an action. Ask yourself: What am I going to do to make this a productive element in my life? Just like you did with your goals in Chapter 4, make each action specific and attainable, and put a time line on it. If you need help changing that stressor into an asset or an incentive, then call on those folks who are on your team. Surround yourself with people who will be honest with you and ask you tough questions to help you deal with the stress.

As you begin changing stressors into incentives, select a simple one to start with. Choose a stressor that will give you a feeling of accomplishment and fulfillment once you've dealt with it. Then, you can move on to more complicated and more cumbersome stressors. Eventually, you will be able to deal with challenges in a quick and efficient manner.

The last suggestion I have to help you deal with stress is to put your progress into words. I'm sure you've heard some of the benefits of talking to yourself, and I don't think that's a bad idea. Verbalize to yourself that you're better after dealing with a stressor than you were before it started. Adversity is not a bad thing in life. I've often said that you never learn to fly around trees until you fly into them. You need to encourage yourself, especially if there are not others around to give you a sense of accomplishment.

One thing to keep in mind is that if you set out to accomplish something every day, which you should, then you must thrive on stress.

This idea always makes me thing of John Smoltz, a pitcher with the Atlanta Braves who still may be the best big-game pitcher in baseball. He always thrived on the challenge and the stress of high-stakes games. For many years, he held the record for playoff game victories. Why? Because those were the games where there was the most stress and, consequently, they were the games he most looked forward to.

Once again positive expectations are the foundation for achievement and quick recovery from adversity. You need to know what you expect of yourself and others in stressful environments, and let others know what you expect of them. It's a major step toward reducing stress in the environment. Not fully knowing what's expected in the workplace creates a very stressful environment, and it causes people to leave jobs every day. Frustration, doubt, and confusion may fuel a stressful situation by activating people's fight-or-flight responses. Clear expectations can prevent this.

We touched on this earlier, but I also recommend that people try to exercise as much as possible, whenever they can. The value of non-competitive exercise in dealing with stress is far too vast to discuss in this chapter. It gives you, in most cases, time alone to think without the clutter that's usually present in personal and professional environments.

Try to keep it fun. Stress can do a number of things *to* us but it can also do a number of things *for* us if we channel it in appropriate ways. You can find the fun side of anything if you take time to do it. I've been in some interesting situations recently that could have caused me to either be very frustrated or to laugh it off and have fun. Balance is a big issue for people with MS, and I recently fell while walking in a city square. I tumbled out into the street, breaking a couple ribs, and I couldn't get up. While I was lying in the street, trying to flag someone down to help me, people were just passing me by and waving back.

I called my son to come and get me, and he and I sat on the sidewalk afterward laughing about what had happened. I told him that so many people were waving at me as they passed.

He pointed out that my long hair gave me a certain look that prevented people from rushing to offer assistance. "Dad, they thought you were homeless and sleeping on the sidewalk."

My response was, "If they had stopped, I would have asked them for money because I knew some of those people."

It was a situation that could have been very frustrating and it could have led to a lot of stress. Instead, I was able to perceive the situation as being somewhat funny. It took me a few weeks to get over the physical problems, but I had recovered from the emotional shock by the time I got up and sat on the curb.

You have to accept the fact that stress is a part of your life, and in many ways stressors can put some levity into your daily life. When it's all said and done, every day should be an exciting day for you.

And I've always thought laughter is one of the quickest and easiest ways to get through stress. To be able to laugh at yourself is, I think, a tremendous asset. Some people are so wrapped up in the corporate structure, numbers, and black-and-white issues in the environment, there's no gray area in their lives, and they find it hard to enjoy every single day, even though, as I've said many, many times, stress is a part of every day; and if it's going to be there, then why not use it to your advantage.

Final Thought

*Thrive on stress and teach your
team to do the same.*

 **Make Stress Work for You**

A. List your top ten stressors.

    1. _____

    2. _____

    3. _____

    4. _____

    5. _____

    6. _____

    7. _____

    8. _____

    9. _____

   10. _____

B. Which of those stressors can and should be aids to your productivity?

    1. _____

    2. _____

    3. _____

    4. _____

C. Indicate the action necessary to convert each stressor on List B to an asset.

    1. _____

    2. _____

    3. _____

    4. _____

D. Of the remaining List A stressors, choose those which can and should be eliminated.

1. _____

2. _____

3. _____

4. _____

E. Indicate the action necessary to eliminate each stressor in List D. Keep the following guidelines in mind:

- Make your actions specific, difficult, and attainable.

- Attach a time frame to each action.

- Evaluate the actions and use them to make stress work for you.

1. _____

2. _____

3. _____

4. _____

Chapter 12

Teach Your Team to Play on the Emotional Edge

We need to play on the emotional edge all day, every day. Leaders don't tell people to relax. Relaxing is the quickest way to shut down your operating system. Instead, true leaders teach people how to recover their edge after facing adversity.

Coaches often talk about playing with emotion and the importance of the mental edge. What do these expressions mean? Can a performer be too emotional? Given a high level of talent, emotion probably does separate the winners from the survivors. Like coaches, leaders need to concentrate every day on developing winners. Emotion can raise talent to an even higher level, not only for individuals but also for teams—sports teams, corporate teams, and family teams.

Uncontrolled emotion, however, can be devastating to performance. Too many times we see the downside of emotion rather than the upside, which is why it's much more common to encourage people to calm down instead of harnessing their emotional energy.

My philosophy is that, for the most part, if you want to win, you never relax during performance. The exception to this is in sport, where taking a calculated mental lapse can help athletes regain their focus. Whether it involves sales, sports, business, or family, act with emotion and perform at as high an emotional level as you can control.

In crisis and conflict, uncontrolled emotions are a serious liability, while controlled emotions can provide a tremendous asset to finding solutions. Emotion is consciously used in recovery from adversity, in focusing techniques, and in concentration. Great players push their emotion to the highest level they can control during performance. Again, this is true in both the sports environment and elsewhere. Getting to the emotional edge is a vital part of this program. To do that, you must first answer the question: What is your emotional edge? On a scale of 1 to 10, what's the optimal level of emotion for top performance. If you're a one, not emotional at all, then you're too relaxed. Lacking emotion means you are not tuned in to what you need to do, so your performance is very low. You tend to make what we call *errors of omission*, which arise when you don't do something you should. This happens because you don't have the selective attention that you need for physical and mental practice, so you will randomly respond to cues, which sometimes help your performance and other times do not.

On the other hand, if you're up around the 10 level, you are too emotional and you tend to make *errors of commission*. You react to every mental cue you get, which causes you to take action even when you shouldn't. Recall the selective attention example of a young child learning to catch a ball and responding to every visual cue that's possible. In addition to watching the ball, the child is gathering information from cars, trees, and other things in the background, which makes it hard to focus. Once the catching skill is developed, then the child recognizes the important cues and locks in on the person throwing the ball, his or her arm, the release, and the ball's flight.

Given the ideal situation, the optimal emotional level will be six or seven. At that point, you're on the emotional edge, at your highest level of performance.

The next questions are: How do you get to that level? How do you sustain it? And if you go over the edge, how do you get back? You will notice that we are not concerned with how a person will relax. The important thing to learn is how to stay at the emotional level of peak performance, not how to back off from it.

First, it's best to gradually scale up to the optimal level of emotion. If you get there first thing in the morning and try to hold it all day, your nervous system won't allow it because it is not possible to hold such a high degree of concentration for a long period of time. People who say they go into the zone for two or three hours are not honest because the human body cannot maintain such deep concentration for more than 45 or 50 seconds. Because of these short bursts of focus, everyone's system needs a break, a mental lapse. The key is to control when you take it as opposed to letting your nervous system decide on its own. I call this the *timed mental lapse*. If you give your system a break of no more than 10 seconds—just enough time to take a deep breath—you can get back to the level of emotion that's going to make you the most productive.

Most people don't raise their emotional level to six or seven for a simple reason: They are afraid. As a society, we're afraid. We're afraid to play or perform on the emotional edge consistently because of what might happen. If you make a commitment to perform at the edge, then you've conceded that at some point you'll go over the edge. Obviously the closer you are to the edge, the more stimuli you will react to emotionally and the greater the chances you will go over the edge.

For example, if you're in heavy traffic in the morning rush and you're already at about a six or seven when some driver cuts in front of you, you're more likely to go over the edge. If you're in the same traffic but you are at a three or a four emotionally when someone cuts you off, your irritation may send your emotional level to a six or seven, but you're still under control.

There is a time to reach the edge and, based on my experience, I am convinced that if you're not willing to go there and take some emotional risk, then you're probably never going to win consistently. You may win on occasion because of your talent, but you won't be able to use your emotions as a supplement, one of the keys that separate the winners from the survivors.

165

Teach Your Team to Play on the Emotional Edge

As a leader, you need to constantly be observing people around you as you do your own job so that you can tell if they're getting too emotional. If they're approaching an 8 or 10 on the emotion scale, you can help them get back to the emotional edge.

Just what does it mean when you go *over the edge*? It means that you've become so intense, so high, that you're out of control emotionally. You're not making conscious decisions at that point because your emotions take over. No one wants to be perceived as being out of control. It makes a person look dangerous. You will be less fearful of going over the edge if you know that you can retreat from that emotional level and if you know how to do so. With that skill in your mental files, you can regain control, so you will be more willing to play or perform on the edge, which is essential to winning at the highest level. If you don't have what's needed to regain control, you're likely to stay relatively far from the edge, which makes it impossible for you to win at the highest level.

How do you get back if you go over the edge? Many people in a corporate environment experience mental tension in the afternoon. It drives people away from having conversations and meetings, and from making conscious and often critical decisions. These people are over the edge emotionally and realize that they will not make good decisions. What they need is to *let their mental tape rewind.*

If you're over the edge, take 10 minutes for a little diversion: close the office door, listen to music, go outside and walk around—all of these activities can help you recharge. I always recommend that people take a power nap. Find a quiet place and get very comfortable, giving yourself the suggestion that you're going to lie down calmly for 10 minutes. It may take several times, but eventually your system will become conditioned and you'll be able to drop off to sleep and wake up 10 minutes later. You will have the energy you need for the rest of the day. This is one way to bring yourself back from the edge. Find a diversion that works to give you a little time out from the work routine.

As a parent, you can take a ride or go shopping for a little while. Divert your mind to break the cycle.

Progressive relaxation is another technique that can bring you back. In times of frustration, some people feel tension in their neck, shoulders, or arms; others experience a headache. Progressive relaxation is the practice of isolating different muscle groups and performing exercises to release the tension. Eight to 10 minutes of these exercises will restore your equilibrium.

Don't fear playing or performing on the edge emotionally; it's the best place to be. The problem arises when you don't take a break. Instead, you may become more frustrated and then go further over the edge.

Athletes illustrate this point, often in visible ways. Some athletes who have had a losing experience on the field will go into the locker room, sit down, and read a book to regain control. But other athletes, after a bad performance, will turn over tables, kick lockers, take baseball bats and attack the plumbing, or throw water coolers onto the playing field. You name it, I've seen it thrown—towels, gloves, helmets, bats, folding chairs. Once I saw football player on the sidelines—he wasn't playing at that moment—go so far over the edge that he ran onto the field and tackled the ball carrier. I've seen out-of-control coaches punch players. I've seen CEOs go into an office and wreck it verbally and physically, ruining a relatively good environment.

If people don't create a way to regain emotional control, then burnout is probably inevitable. Imagine a person in a job that is not going well; each day drives the emotional level higher and higher. People call home to say they'll be late for dinner because they feel they need to add hours to the day. If they usually work 10 hours, they add three more. If they usually work five days a week, they start working six. Rather than analyzing the 10 hours of work and trying to get more out of that time, they set themselves up to spend two to three additional hours on emotional endeavors, not productive activity. How many of those people eventually don't call home anymore because it's assumed they're going to be late for dinner.

The backlash comes in the worker's personal life, as more tension and emotion build up each time he or she isn't home for dinner. When you add two or three hours to your working day and then make it part of your lifestyle, you have stolen that time. You've stolen it from your family, your friends, and your leisure time. You've stolen that time from the very side of life that is your motive for your work in the first place.

That is why I keep asking the question: *Why do you do what you do?* If you don't have an answer, then taking time from your personal life is a nonissue. If you do understand why you do what you do and still steal time, then your frustrations eventually will drive you from your job. You'll wake up one morning and hate your work because it has stolen your personal life.

One of the major responsibilities of leadership is pretty common-sense. It's to make sure that your people understand why they do what they do, understand that for everything that's professionally significant there has to be something personally significant in their lives—and sometimes you need to take those people aside and remind them of this. If you keep working long hours and the mental tape keeps getting tighter and tighter, eventually you're going to wake up one morning and, while you're in the shower, you're going to hear a strange flap, flap, flap. That's the sound of your mental tape self-destructing. And you can't replace it. When it's gone, it's gone. That's the worst-case scenario.

You have to make a conscious effort to play with emotion every day but to keep it under control consciously. Before you get caught up in your job or sport or anything else, stop and think about the ramifications and the toll that uncontrolled emotion takes on your life. You have to understand and recognize the symptoms of going over the edge to know where that point is for you because it's different for everyone. Mentally record feelings during performance when you are successful.

Do this immediately afterward before you leave the environment. Mentally replay what you just did and store that successful experience. When you store it, you not only input the mechanics but also the emotions of the experience. This enables you to know when you're reaching that emotional level again. Visualize this again and again and again. Repeat the process until the emotions are stored with the mechanics.

A few years ago I worked with a pro baseball player who was a great hitter but he was inconsistent. Sometimes he was terrific, and other times he was terrible. When I met him, he'd fallen into a bad slump because he was trying *not* to miss, *not* to make mistakes, *not* to look bad as opposed to swinging to hit the ball to be successful.

We talked about his problem. "Can you remember one time when you hit the ball and it was like music? When it was vintage you? When it was perfect and everything was place?" I asked him.

Suddenly that big athlete came to the edge of his seat and his eyes began to well with tears. "Yeah," he said, "it was against Philadelphia, seventh inning. It was cold that night. We were behind 3-2. The count went to 3-1, and I hit a fastball. It was inside, and I hit it, and it didn't feel like I hit it, but it went over the fence. It was a great feeling. We won." And he kept on talking about that hit.

"How many times have you thought about that hit since then?" I asked him.

He looked surprised. "You know, this is the first time."

The information had been stored mentally, and when the hitter recalled the performance, he replayed not only the mechanics but also the emotional feeling he had. Within a couple of days the hitter came out of his slump. He started hitting as he had before. It wasn't because he changed the mechanics of hitting; it was because of his ability to recall the winning emotional level that enabled him to repeat the performance.

You can do that in every walk of life. You always store the information, whether it's good or bad. It's just a matter of finding it and pulling it up. Although it's not an easy task, the more often you retrieve the information, the easier it becomes. The rule is that before any performance or activity, you visualize a previous similar experience. It will serve as an incentive or a motivator and also raise your emotional level to the desired point. Then if you should go over the edge during a performance, all you need to do is take a deep breath, visualize, and return to the optimal level. You can do that in a matter of seconds.

Particularly important here is to apply this sport concept to business. If you're getting ready to have a meeting, pull up a memory of a good meeting you've had before. Recall it in your mind. Play it through in real time. Anticipate questions and answers you will face in the meeting to come. And after this process, you'll be more comfortable and closer to the emotional edge.

Remember, you do not want to relax and fall all the way down to a one on the emotional scale and then, immediately before the performance, try to climb back up to a six or a seven. Unfortunately, most people engage in yo-yo emotions. They spend most of the day going up and down so they're emotionally fatigued by the time it's over.

Everyone has what is considered a normal daily activation level. Here's how it works: The emotional arousal level goes up to a certain point when you get up in the morning, dress, and head for work or another activity. The level varies from person to person, but you work off that base all day. It goes up and down, but stays close to that starting range. If an important telephone call comes in, suddenly you have to elevate your emotional level because it results in better, quicker decisions. After the call ends, the emotions drop back to the base level and you relax. Then, you have to attend a meeting and your emotional level rises again, but it returns to the base level afterward. The result is mental and emotional fatigue, not because you went back to the base level but because you had to raise the level to make important decisions. It makes sense to go to the edge and stay there, eliminating the need to spend so much time and emotional energy going up and down. Staying on the edge, of course, is not a static situation. You'll fluctuate up and down a little, but you'll be able to hold a relatively clear emotional line all day once you have mastered this technique.

Most amateur golf matches, for example, are lost after the 15th hole, not because of a bad shot but because of bad decisions. That happens because people work so hard mentally during the first 15 holes that they're fatigued going into 16. A quick remedy for those of you who are golfers is to never lock in on a shot until you get to it. Don't waste emotion when you're walking to the shot. Don't waste emotion when you're riding the cart. You lock in, you select a club, you hit it, and you save tons of emotion if you practice that.

Note: You must understand a very important effect of staying on the edge. You'll be perceived as a threat to people who are relatively relaxed and never rise above a two or three on the emotional scale. That means you have to be totally committed to playing on the edge. You also need to feel good about being up there and winning. Eventually, you'll reach the point where you're able to go to the edge and stay as long as you want. That's when you're going to do things that other people cannot do and achieve things they dare not try. This does not always create admiration and respect. In fact, it often engenders envy and contempt.

There's no question that when we talk about emotion we're basically talking about anxiety. By definition, anxiety is a generalized feeling of fear or worry about things that might happen or of the possible consequences of the events. Unlike stress, which was discussed in Chapter 11, anxiety is sometimes hard to get a handle on even though we talk a lot about it. If this emotion were defined in stages, the first stage would be feeling nervous. The majority of people say their greatest fear is speaking in front of groups. If you've done this, you know you get a rush through your system. Your voice may change. You get muscle tension.

Teach Your Team to Play on the Emotional Edge

The second level of anxiety is tension. It may result from a lack of knowledge or worry over the consequences of your upcoming actions.

The third level is fear. It stems from a perceived threat and can drive your performance higher until it reaches a certain level. Then it can drive you out of the optimal zone. This level is often referred to as being *psyched up* and sometimes *psyched out*, having butterflies and choking. If you reach that level and do not take control of your emotions, then you reach the panic point. That's the most serious level of anxiety.

The best antidote is patience, which is very difficult to practice if you're in a panic. Unless you have a vehicle in place to control your emotions, you can develop phobias that may drive you completely out of a particular environment.

In working with athletes, I encounter this question constantly: Do you motivate athletes in sport psychology? To the contrary, as I've said before in this book, I've never in 45 years tried to motivate an athlete. In fact, I spend most of my time trying to get athletes down to the edge as opposed to up. Most of them are already motivated; it's a prerequisite to being where they are.

In sports, a lot of players are known as *practice players*. They perform like champions in practice but don't play well during the game because of their anxiety level. This is related to the fear of failure. The fear has crossed the point from being an incentive to performance and has become a detriment. It's common for aggressive athletes to work on raising the anxiety level of opponents to drive down their performance level, and many times it works. Of course, it can also have the reverse effect. Raising the anxiety level can actually improve performance, so players role the dice when they employ that device in a contest.

You have probably seen that kind of psychological competition quite often. It's the manipulation of anxiety levels by fans against the opposing team and between colleagues, and siblings, and even parents and children. Nothing physical happens, but there is a play on the anxiety level. For instance, when a game-winning field goal is about to be attempted, the opposing team will call a time-out to create time for the kicker's anxiety level to rise, maybe impeding his execution. It's also common in sales presentations. Some people want to go first while others prefer to go last. It depends on where they are psychologically and emotionally and what they believe is most beneficial to them.

Look for telltale signs from your mental files to alert you when you're not where you want to be emotionally or you're over the edge. One sign is less efficiency in your performance. Another is freezing up in high-power situations. Forgetting assignments, losing touch, and other negative side effects are also common.

In baseball, for example, a player may lose the feel for the ball, and proneness to injury may also be a sign of an ineffective emotional level. Athletes who want to play but are afraid of failure will find a way to be injured just before they are to perform. A minor-league pitcher with whom I worked had major-league talent but every time he got called up, he would get injured. This happened three times. First, he turned his ankle; the next time he ran into a wall; and finally he hurt his back. He had a good career as a minor-league survivor but never pitched in the majors. It was the result of his fear of failure, another emotional issue. He was afraid to win, even though he wanted to be a great competitor. He feared that if he won, his accountability would increase, expectations would go up, and so would his responsibility. Surviving was more comfortable than truly winning at what he wanted to do. It was very sad to see in such a talented person.

Every day in the corporate environment, leaders must constantly be aware of whether people have a fear of success or a fear of failure. One of the telltale signs of a fear of success is that a person will perform at an acceptable level but never take a risk. In contrast, people who have a fear of failure will accept challenges that are so easy that if they're basically breathing they can succeed. Many people encounter the fear of success or failure, the loss of emotional control, or ignorance

173

Teach Your Team to Play on the Emotional Edge

of their optimal level of emotions. These controllable shortcomings cause a constant rising and falling in performance. You can be a 10 emotionally today and down to 1 tomorrow, then back up to 10 the next day. This is frustrating, but you learn to understand your emotional levels and gain control of them. You cannot only empower yourself but also help others to grow stronger and better, especially those closest to you every day. It takes time, effort, and sufficient practice to build confidence. It's very difficult to build if you never get to play or perform.

The key is to motivate people to reach their optimal level, which comes from creating an environment that's conducive to performance; maintaining a consistent, sustainable emphasis on performance; and setting realistic goals but making them tough enough to stretch your system. As we talked about in Chapter 4, they should be specific but attainable, and you should set time frames to reach them. Anxiety is good when it's under control. You want your performance anxiety to be relatively high as you anticipate an upcoming event, then you want it to slide back a little as you step up to the task at hand. Once you get started, it will increase as a natural consequence of your actions and situation. Your post-performance anxiety may rise or stay even.

A vital part of dealing with anxiety and emotions is your team, both the personal and professional. This chapter ends with some practical exercises. Have your team practice some situations that artificially create pressure. Use verbal and nonverbal positive reinforcement to build confidence and self-concept in people.

Final Thought

Use emotion as a supplement to performance.
Play on the edge.

Teach Your Team to Play on the Edge

List the personal situations that create pressure for you.

1. _____
2. _____
3. _____
4. _____
5. _____

List verbal reinforcements that create confidence for you.

1. _____
2. _____
3. _____
4. _____
5. _____

List nonverbal reinforcements that create confidence for you.

1. _____
2. _____
3. _____
4. _____
5. _____

List the professional situations that create pressure for your team.

1. _____
2. _____
3. _____
4. _____
5. _____

List verbal reinforcements that create confidence for your team.

1. _____
2. _____
3. _____
4. _____
5. _____

List nonverbal reinforcements that create confidence for your team.

1. _____
2. _____
3. _____
4. _____
5. _____

Chapter 13

Recover More Quickly from Adversity and Win

L earn how to recover more quickly from adversity. Corporate feedback reflects an extremely strong interest in this topic. Simply put, those who recover more quickly win, while those who don't merely survive, especially in sales-based companies.

The word *recovery* usually conjures up thoughts of overcoming an extremely negative condition or circumstance. Usually when we talk about recovery, people assume it involves terrible problems or even tragedy. That's not necessarily the case. Everyone is confronted daily with situations from which they need to recover in order to retain a desirable level of performance.

In business and personal life, people constantly recover from conflict, crises, and stressors. Salespeople have to recover from daily rejections. Several times a day at least a parent must recover from the frustrations of rearing children and carrying out the normal routines of running a household. Athletes have to recover from setbacks and lapses. Hitters must recover from slumps. Pitchers have to recover from bad pitches. Recovery is a necessary part of every walk of life.

It's critical that you learn to recover from adversity and to do so quickly. This ability separates talented people who win consistently from those who win casually, lose, or just survive. If you know the technique and you have a process in your mental files that enables you to speed up your recovery from adversity, then you're going to perform better over a longer period of time than people who don't have the recovery technique or process. Quick recovery from adversity is a critical skill personally and professionally.

Nearly everyone with talent will win on occasion. Sometimes people are described as winning by accident, and that happens too. Given the right circumstances, you can win if you just show up, but this is not the case when it comes to regular, reliable success. Talent alone does not ensure winning, although it is a prerequisite. But you also have to be totally committed to what you're doing and what you want to achieve. Granted, part of the equation for success is being in the right place at the right time and getting the right breaks. But this kind of good fortune alone will not guarantee success without the other parts of the equation. Over the long term, you must have the capability to recover from misfortune or adversity.

As a leader, you need to be very perceptive of adversity and assume that another person's struggle may seem trivial to you, but it's very significant to them. We cannot judge people by how they react to different situations. We have to help them put a program in place mentally so that, regardless of the severity of the adversity, they can recover quickly.

In my judgment, the speed of recovery ranks among the most important variables for success, yet it is seldom discussed in books. If you have talent, then you will recover in time, but the key is learning to reduce how long it takes. There are two ways to do this. The first is recognizing adversity when it begins to appear, so you have enough time to counter it. The second is, when you hit bottom, learning to return to the level where you were previously. Even though you always play to win, it's healthy to lose sometimes so that you learn to recover. While losing is not what we set out to do, it presents us with an opportunity to improve ourselves, and that is a valuable part of life.

You will find losing to be an almost insurmountable barrier to performance if you're so talented that you've never felt the need to learn mental skills for fast recovery. Unfortunately, as in the case of some athletes whom I've worked with and known, people refuse to concede that adversity could ever rear its ugly head in their lives. That attitude presents a very difficult problem indeed.

A friend who was an outstanding high school football coach compiled an enviable record of 54 consecutive victories, which won him a place in the coaches hall of fame. His players never lost a game from the eighth grade until they graduated from high school. Many of the youngsters then signed major college scholarships.

But something unexpected happened. After a year or two, many of those players showed up back in their hometown. They'd quit their teams—not because they lacked talent or intelligence but because they had begun to lose games, make mistakes, and not perform as well as they had in high school. Because of the extraordinary success they had in their school years, their ability to recover was minimal. Up until that point it hadn't been a skill they needed to learn.

Take the case of a college pitcher who was signed by a pro team in his senior year in college. He had a record of 15 wins and no losses, making him a top draft choice. When he arrived at spring training, he discovered everyone on the team was just as good as he was, so that even when he was pitching well he wasn't winning all the time. As a result, he suffered from terrible anxiety problems that forced him to quit after less than one year. It was not due to any lack of talent; it stemmed from his inability to recover from adversity. He had never learned how to recover when he made a bad pitch or lost a game. Again, recovery is critical to sustaining performance and to winning.

The same principle applies to employees who keep their jobs after a company has gone through reorganization and cutbacks. In such situations, more efforts should be made to teach the retained employees to recover more quickly from adversity. This, too, is critical for the company. These employees will be required to do more work, to increase their productivity, and in some cases to give up the proper balance in their lives because of greater demands on them, creating

Recover More Quickly from Adversity and Win

additional adversity from which they will need to recover. They also face another challenge. They no longer have as strong a support system because so many of their fellow workers are gone. The company does not have the luxury of its employees making a relatively slow, deliberate recovery; that chance is gone. Business continues, so a quick recovery is required.

How do you learn to recover quickly? The first step in this process is to accept that adversity is real. It is a daily experience in life in most environments.

Next, you must assume you will be better by having gone through the adversity recovery process. You will learn from the experience and discover that you are a stronger person than you thought. And in the process you will prove to yourself that you can deal with conflict, and you will learn that adversity is not going to stand in the way of your goals.

If you are to recover quickly, you must avoid what I call the *dark tunnels*. These are parts of your mind that are filled with memories of your past mistakes. One of the worst habits to have is spending too much time replaying mistakes over and over, concentrating on avoiding them instead of focusing on what you should be doing well. It's good to review your mistakes briefly to develop a goal-based plan that will make you better. Otherwise dwelling on mistakes is like drinking poison every day. This approach makes it impossible to recover and return to a successful level of winning. At that point, the only option is survival, and unfortunately many people begin to feel complacent about where they are.

Think about how long it takes you to recover from adverse situations. How long do you carry the baggage around? If you are in sales and you make a presentation at 9:00 in the morning and get kicked out at 9:05, how long is it before you're back to being yourself again? Do you need three hours? Four hours? During the time it took you to recover, how many people did you turn off or upset? How many sales calls did you miss? How many potential closings? If you're honest with yourself, you'll find that adversity costs you significantly, not only in terms of financial reward but also personally, in terms of your relationships with other people.

If, as a leader, you make a controversial and difficult decision, how long do you dwell on it before you move ahead? Winners recover quickly. Winning hitters recover between swings of the bat, not between times at the plate. Winning salespeople recover between sales calls, not between days.

Recovering quickly is difficult, without question. The mechanics may be easy, but it is difficult to sustain. You must make a daily commitment to play to win; you have to want to recover.

Certain things are necessary in order to understand the seven-step recovery process. First, you have to define winning. This enables you to know when you have fully recovered. For a golfer I worked with, poor putting had become his adversity. In this case winning meant standing over the ball confidently, seeing the line from the ball to the cup, and stroking the putt with certainty. It was a matter of loss of emotional control, and we worked on how he could recover it. Finally he reached the point when, if he prepared to putt and didn't have a significant feeling, he stepped back, took a deep breath, and visualized a good putt he had made before. That restored the appropriate emotional level, and he performed better than he had in months.

Second, you must learn to recognize the signs of adversity. It does not always hit you in the face. There are subtle clues such as beginning to feel uncomfortable in a task, becoming anxious during performance, and feeling too much tension. You become unsure of yourself and are tentative in your presentation. When one or more of these symptoms appear, you need to start the recovery process. A typical reaction to adversity is to ignore it and attempt to move on. However, this can result in a worst-case scenario that requires much more time to recover than if you act quickly when you encounter difficulties, mistakes, and failure.

Consider another example from golfing. Some players I have counseled called me for assistance after they failed to make several tournaments or performed poorly when they made the cut. If they had sought help after missing the first cut or after the first three bad holes, then their recovery would have been accomplished within hours; instead, it took weeks.

Players who want to correct things in their game after years of doing them the wrong way expect to fix the problem in one or two days. Recovery doesn't work that way. Think of performance problems as analogous to addiction. The longer you smoke cigarettes, the longer it will take you to break free of the craving and recover to the nonsmoker life.

Third, you must learn to visualize, as discussed in Chapter 9. You have to see yourself mentally managing adversity and succeeding. It is essential that you store successful performances in your mental file. Any time you pull up a previously well-executed meeting or shot, you're adding to the positive file in your mind and you should be able to recall them whenever you choose.

These positive entry behaviors must be on file for use when needed. On occasion you should mentally recall a brush with adversity and then follow it with visualization exercises of how you successfully managed to overcome it. The most important variable is experience. You can develop a pattern of recovery through visualization. Relatively basic visualization facilitates your learning to focus during adversity. Focusing enables you to develop a plan to pursue success and to recover.

Fourth, selective attention is a prerequisite to recovery. As we discussed in Chapter 10, selective attention helps you maintain your focus, which is crucial to recovery. To use a well-worn expression, it's about keeping your eye on the ball, which, in sports that use balls, can be taken literally. A golfer who hits into the sand must focus very selectively to get out of the sand. This used to cause me terrible anxiety on the golf course. "I'll never get out of the sand," I thought. Finally, a teacher told me to focus on hitting an inch or two behind the ball to get out of the sand. It works, and now the sand traps don't raise my anxiety level at all.

If there is something that automatically causes adversity for you, then you need to confront it head on and develop actions to deal with it. The next time it comes up, you'll be able to recover.

Fifth, you must realize that winners are either very popular or very unpopular in their environments, neighborhoods, or hometowns. While some people look at winners as heroes, others may be jealous or resentful. Survivors may be more popular because the winners set a standard that survivors do not appreciate or accept. You may find that you're bucking the system when you try to win.

That happened to a fifth grader who was very bright. He set a pace that was uncomfortable for his classmates. They began to intimidate the youngster, make fun of him, and ridicule him every day. The student soon became frustrated and confused. His grades fell, and then his tormentors left him alone because he was no longer a threat. But three years later, the boy is in a different school where intelligence is respected by his peers, so he has a positive attitude and his grades have improved. The recovery's been a long, slow process, and if he'd been removed from the negative environment sooner, his recovery would have been much quicker.

Sixth, you must understand how your winning affects other people during the recovery process. Other people must become involved in helping you until you can once again be a contributing member of a team. This is universal in the sports, business, and home environments.

Seventh, the recovery process requires patience. Obviously this is true of our physical health, yet some athletes and other people are so impatient and aggressive by nature that they try to shorten the natural healing time. You need to be patient. Sometimes you'll find that this is the most difficult part of learning and practicing recovery. In sports, post-injury patience is a worthy challenge.

Recover More Quickly from Adversity and Win

When you've assumed a leadership position in a corporate environment, common sense tells you that people look to you when they try to recover. So pace yourself; even though you're trying to recover quickly, there's a certain amount of patience that will enable you to be more effective. When your people see it, they will respond and follow your lead. You must show patience in helping people to recover or change behaviors. This support is valuable for employee retention.

Parents in particular must understand that children don't change overnight. Sometimes it's one step forward and two steps back before the pattern is reversed and progress can be made.

Now let's talk a bit about the mechanics of recovery and the all-important perspective you have of the process. You're not recovering *from* something, you're recovering *to* good performance. Never run away from things. When something negative happens, back off mentally and visualize yourself performing the task or engaging in an activity correctly. If it is a conversation that didn't go well, immediately afterward take a few minutes to yourself and replay the conversation. Don't wait. Determine what went well, what could have gone better, and how you will improve the next time. By the time that happens, there will be little if any adversity because you have made the corrections mentally beforehand.

If you don't have a video recorder available to provide you with footage of an actual replay, then when you engage in an activity and do it well, take a few minutes and replay that process in detail. If it was your best performance, whether a speech or a sales call, a decision or a sports skill, then immediately afterward take a few seconds and replay it so you can store that correct performance in your mental file to be called up when needed. Every time you do this you're storing behaviors that you will recall to recover when necessary.

In your free time, visualize your past successes. This exercise repeated over and over will enable you to achieve faster recovery from the negative impact of adversity. Think about how bad adversity tastes. If you do not want to face the negative effects of adversity, now you know the quickest relief comes from what you have stored mentally and you use it to work on recovery. Use the worksheet that follows to remind yourself of the steps that can help you to recover from adversity, both professionally and personally.

Sprint Cup NASCAR driver Tony Stewart is exceptionally talented, determined, and totally committed. He began to experience adversity on the track, which spilled over into his personal life. To be successful in both environments required two behavioral styles. Aggression that was rewarded on the track was criticized off the track. Luckily, he is very bright, perceptive, and compassionate, and was able to take advantage of these strengths to recover quickly in six steps.

First, he recognized the negative consequences of his reactions to adversity.

Second, he made a conscious decision to learn how to recover more quickly.

Third, he put a plan in place and surrounded himself with people who understood adversity and how to recover quickly.

Fourth, he learned that a change in behavior would cause others to be suspicious. He learned to sustain this new behavior even under skeptical eyes until people realized he had sincerely changed.

Fifth, he learned that there are people who are attracted to adversity, those who like to pile on when a person's down, and he eliminated them from his life.

Six, he learned that emotion is a tremendous asset, and he used his edge to win the NASCAR championship that year.

It's very interesting that the bottom line to the whole process in working with Tony Stewart was to get him to spend his energy on things he controlled and to let the rest go.

Recover More Quickly from Adversity and Win

Any good leader knows that if you're going to be effective, you've got to control what you can control and let the rest go. You've got to have people on your team who you let do their jobs. People are going to make mistakes, but they're going to make mistakes trying to get better, not trying to avoid failure.

Remember, the key to success is not recovery. Everyone will recover over time if they have talent. The key to success is speed of recovery.

Final Thought

Quick recovery separates winners from survivors.

 **Recover from Adversity**

1. Review your assets and liabilities from Chapter 2.

2. Analyze the adversity in the present situation.

3. Review the goals you are trying to achieve.

4. Determine which assets can be used to offset this adversity and achieve the desired result.

5. Write down specific actions that will lead you to success.

6. Prioritize these actions and begin to recover.

7. Evaluate your recovery for speed, effectiveness, and efficiency.

Recover More Quickly from Adversity and Win

Chapter 14

Help Your Team to Achieve Balance

B alance is more than just a physical parameter impacting performance. Winners interpret balance to mean much more than physical equilibrium. Balance is a concept that has become a major issue in
the lives of most people. It's a topic at many conventions and is
especially relevant to employees who are married or have families.
Most of the time, the two sides of the scale are work life and personal
life. For leaders, this is perhaps the most important chapter in the book
because without balance in your own life, it's very difficult to help your
colleagues achieve it in theirs.

There are also very specific issues of balance within your personal
life. If you're a parent, how do you balance time with your spouse and
your children? How do you balance time between the children? How do
you find personal time for yourself?

If you are a management professional or a leader in the corporate
environment, your work life can also be a juggling act. How do you
balance your job within the parameters of your environment? Do
you push some employees too hard while neglecting others? What
if you have one person who's not motivated and five people who are
self-motivated? Do you spend more time motivating the one person or
should you be more concerned with the five good people?

It's critical that a manager understand balance in order to deal with
employees successfully. Many companies have committed a fatal error
in thinking that everyone can be motivated and the same methods

apply universally. You must understand that, in every day of your life, balance is a challenge because you are a leader.

How many people today work longer hours than in past years, as evidenced by the number of corporate re-engineering announcements and cutbacks in workforces? Companies expect more productivity from fewer people. That usually means more time away from home for employees.

Most people in high-productivity environments work longer hours than they did in the past. It's not necessarily a negative development. You should work longer hours when you absolutely must, but doing so should not become a permanent part of your lifestyle.

Achieving balance seems to be an impossible task for many professional people and for many parents as well. Spend some time around moms and dads who have three to four children. You realize it's incredibly difficult for them to keep balance within the home. They may feel as if they never have any time for themselves, as a couple or individually.

Even children's lives are at risk of being poorly balanced. How many obligations do children have these days? When I was a youngster, we played a sport or two and went to school. Now there are so many extracurricular activities and school activities that children have a hard time maintaining balance in their lives.

Whenever I include a balance component in my program, it generates more comments than any other single segment of the presentation. People are hungry for balance, and they are asking for help. This is a dramatic change from just a few years ago and, as a result, I've come to believe that we as a society are beginning to understand the importance of balance in our lives. We are beginning to understand fulfillment, meeting our basic needs, and helping those around us meet theirs. I think we're making progress.

If we look at the quality of time as opposed to the number of hours, which I think is necessary, how many of us have lost our balance? I find that an alarming percentage of successful people in high positions in the community, civic clubs, and the corporate world are unhappy and unfulfilled because they've lost their balance, and they don't really have any idea about how to correct the issue. They work longer and harder, and rest on the excuse that they're financially providing for their family, which is their job.

Winning demands intensive training and devotion to a daily routine. That takes a commitment to work. Incredible amounts of time are required to achieve perfection or high levels of performance. Therefore, most of our time is spent on work. That fact alone doesn't mean that you lack good balance. It's the quality of the time spent that is a critical issue. People who are devoted and good at what they do are usually going to work long hours, but again, the key to balance is the quality of time spent.

A challenging assignment for me was working with a group of promising young sales managers in management development sessions. We met every month, first as a group and then individually. In the one-on-one meetings, conversations often turned to the issue of professional versus personal interest. Over and over I heard people complain, "I have no personal time. I don't have time for my children." Balance was a major issue in the lives of these young professionals. As is so often the case these days, their goal was to work long and hard and retire at 35. Some of them worked seven days a week, sometimes 15 to 18 hours a day, which left no time for family, friends, or themselves. Paradoxically, productivity declined as they spent more hours at work because their focus wasn't as sharp. This reinforced the cycle of working more to get everything done, and a very simple philosophy prevailed: Need more money, work longer hours.

I used the strategies in this book to help them be more aware of where they were, where they wanted to go, whom they wanted to take with them, and when, realistically, they wanted to get there. We also set goals for the personal side of life. Each person kept an hourly log for a

Help Your Team to Achieve Balance

week to determine how time was spent and what was accomplished. We were looking for common threads running across every day, similar tasks at similar times and so forth. I was looking for time slots for self-reward as well as time slots for learning opportunities. For some in the group I had to actually plug in family time until they began to understand the value of spending time at home.

The good news is that after three months of working together, every person in the group summarized the course with comments about balance: "I'm grateful for these meetings because I have balance in my life," wrote one individual. "I finally feel good about me and about what I do, and about my role professionally and personally," another wrote.

I've seen major-league athletes with tremendous talents never make the grade and even be released by teams because they never learned to balance playing the game with the things that are peripheral to it. When that happens, it may be too late to save a career in sports or in business, or to salvage personal relationships. I've worked with athletes who have played better after dealing with things peripheral to the game.

When rookie players come to the major leagues, I tell them this in our first conversation: You can play or you wouldn't be at this level. Now your major issue is learning how to live at the major-league level. In other words, learn how to balance your life. Learn how to rest and get enough sleep. Learn when to do each of the things you have to do. It takes some athletes a couple years to do that.

Start-up businesses in the digital age are especially susceptible to being out of balance. The lure of the prospective payoff at the back end is so great that people work a staggering number of hours up front, and they're willing to roll the dice, knowing the business may not succeed.

My question to the start-up workaholics is this: What have you done to your life and what have you done to your personal relationships if there is no payoff? You should never put your entire life in your job. You must never give up the personal things in your life. Always retain quality of life on the personal side. Just because you're at home a number of hours doesn't mean that you have balance. You have to be there not only physically, but also mentally to count it as quality time. That doesn't mean you have to plan a lot of activities. It's enough to stay at home and enjoy the company of your family and friends. You need to have that in order to say that you truly have balance.

In speaking at conventions when I emphasize the urgency of gaining balance and maintaining it, some people get very uncomfortable. From my observation, most of the ones who don't like the idea are at the executive level of their company, but I don't think those people are leaders in most cases anyway.

At a team-building seminar for a major consulting firm, I talked with a senior partner of the firm before the seminar in order to evaluate the topics and the points to be covered. "I saw your videotape," he told me, "and I loved your material, but I want you to avoid talking about that balance issue with my people."

"Sure," I laughed, thinking he was kidding.

The grim look on the guy's face told me he was not kidding. "I don't want my people thinking that when they leave the meeting with you today," he said, "that they will be free to leave the office before eight o'clock at night. I don't want them to think that, for the sake of this balance you're talking about, they don't have to come in on weekends either."

It was sad, but that is how people are used many times. When I talked with his employees, many of them were young, single, high-energy people right out of college. I had a very difficult time omitting the part about balance, which those people needed so badly. Even though I didn't talk about it as a topic, I slipped in some references to balance within other topics. I felt an obligation to do that whether or not I got invited for another seminar at that firm.

The long and the short of it is pretty simple. Adding hours to the day is not the answer. There isn't much evidence that if people work

193

Help Your Team to Achieve Balance

13 hours versus 10 they will be more productive. The key is to explore ways to get the productivity needed within the time frame planned for the work.

A corporate executive once told me he was proud to say that he'd spent 16 to 18 hours a day doing his job his whole career. "Fine," I replied, and left it at that. But I don't know that there's any job worth 18 hours a day of your life or one that would even require close to 18 hours a day. It does not make sense to routinely add hours to the day.

If business is tough, your employer may call you in and say, "We need to get more done. We need to increase business." Immediately, as a leader, your tendency will be to add hours onto your team's schedule. That's not the answer. If they're already working eight hours, they start working eleven. If they're working five days a week, they add a day and work six. Then on the seventh day, they're mentally still at work even though physically they're off. These workaholics never stop to examine the 10- or 11-hour days that they work. They never learn to find more productive time within a normal workday. Yet a great amount of research indicates that there are only 7 or 8 hours of productivity within those 10 hours. I would suspect the same would hold true for 12- or 13-hour days. It's like stretching four years of college into six. You stay busy and get the degree two years later.

Think about what is happening in your life. If you're working a tremendous number of hours and you miss the things your children do growing up, do you not regret that as time passes? You may not hear your child say the first word or take the first step or catch the first ball or get the first hit or bring home the first A or get the first black eye or have the first emotional squabble or the first dance. Firsts don't happen twice. Of course, you can't possibly see everything your child does for the first time, but you should make an effort to do as much as you can with your children in terms of quality of time so that you don't miss all those things. Think about it. You can't go back and walk and talk about things you missed with your children once they're adults because they know you weren't there, so you need to make a commitment to attend to the important things in life, whether they involve your children, your spouse, or someone else.

Most of the time when balance is lost, it's gone before you realize it. Then retrieving your balance is extremely difficult. You get into a routine, get comfortable, and it's very difficult to change.

Regaining balance becomes essentially a behavioral change, the toughest change for an adult. Changing behavior with respect to balance may not always mean personal interest versus professional interest. The issue may be balance within the job itself. For example, professional golfers have a tendency to overpractice. They don't have much balance between the physical and mental practice. Hitters who are in a slump have a tendency to go to practice early every day and hit too many balls as opposed to balancing out the physical practice with the mental practice. If you're a hitter and you're in a slump, take a couple of days off. If you're a golfer and you hit three great shots in a row, then go on to the next club and practice with it. Hit three shots and then walk away.

How do you achieve balance? Well, the first thing you do is set aside time. You must feel comfortable about giving up this time. If balance is based solely on the amount of time spent and not the quality of time—and in the beginning this often holds true—it's worse than no balance at all.

I once worked with a tremendous young tennis player. I had no doubt she would win a college scholarship and rise in professional competition. She was not only a great athlete but she also had a winning personality. She was warm and unassuming. During her matches, we encouraged her parents, or at least one for every competition, to attend and give moral support. This became a major problem. The father didn't want to take time from work because that was his life, but since we made it a requirement he showed up at the matches. He was so uncomfortable taking the time out of his work that his behavior became

Help Your Team to Achieve Balance

erratic. He became verbally abusive to his daughter and her opponents. On one occasion he threw a chair onto the tennis court. Finally the officials banned him from the matches. Although I didn't talk with him afterward, I'm sure he felt better when he was at work because that was where he wanted to be and he didn't need to make excuses anymore. When he spent time at the matches it fell far short of genuine balance because he was not there in a supportive fashion. The quality of the time he spent ranked lower than 0 on a scale of 1 to 10 because it was a negative experience for everyone.

The girl's mother was asked to fill the gap. She began attending the matches, but this took time from her social activities, which she felt were the most important things in her life. Her obsession with social doings probably exceeded her husband's obsession with work. She became rowdier than he had been, and as a result, both she and her daughter then were banned from the tennis court and the park. That father and mother grudgingly spent a quantity of time with no quality attached, and it significantly impacted their family in a negative way. Their daughter never played tennis again. This illustrates that time spent is not the same as quality time.

A growing number of businesspeople and employees are attempting to find balance by telecommuting. Some work at home two or three days a week while others do their job almost exclusively at home, but there is a misconception that if you are in your home office that you automatically have balance. Many times just the opposite happens. Though your children may be present in the "office" with you, they are not likely spending any quality time with you. You might assume that you have quality time for yourself because you are in a better work environment. Often, the opposite is true. When you have your workplace at home, you may spend more time working than you would if you were in a corporate environment. As a result, your balance is actually worse than it would have been if you didn't have the home office. You need to still pick your times when you are there and when you are not there. It's virtually impossible to get quality time if you don't designate specific work hours.

You need to learn to manage your time wisely and then to balance it. Once you have developed an effective time-management plan, then you're in the swing of the process. You'll find you're better organized, more productive, and have more time to be proactive toward balance. You must accept the idea that time pressure will not end as long as you are a normally functioning individual. You can come in early, work late, work on weekends, and think about work when you're not working, but the time crunch will always be a challenge. Time management can be stressful, but that provides you with what you need to thrive. The advantages of thriving on stress are covered in Chapter 11.

As a leader, it's virtually impossible to help people with balance if you don't have balance in your own life, so this chapter is meant to help leaders develop the skills before teaching them to their colleagues. In order to develop balance that we can maintain, we must recognize some common barriers to time management. Here's a starter list:

- Interruptions: telephones, computers, the unexpected
- Trivia
- Poor communication of decisions
- Other people's schedules
- Lack of respect for your time
- Environmental factors
- Work versus home expectations

You can start by controlling the controllable factors. This is accomplished when you follow these steps:

Step one: Keep a log for at least one week. List the things you do each day. Attach a time to each task. You will discover that your productive times will be very similar from day to day. You'll also discover that conceptual, creative productive times will be consistent across days. The first step will help you determine when you are most productive.

Step two: Select one hour per day for a few days. Plan productive execution during that hour and evaluate your productivity.

Step three: Share what you're doing with those people who influence your time. This is absolutely necessary as a leader. In order to achieve your desired time management and balance, mutual respect for each other's approach must be developed.

Continue to follow these steps, gradually increasing the amount of time you consciously manage. Be committed to leaving free time each day to do nothing. Once you are comfortable with what you're able to accomplish in a typical day, you might start making a to-do list nightly for the next day. It's essential that you start each list with things that you can and will accomplish early the next morning. This approach simply gives you momentum to get through your list.

I recommend people make two lists, one for the things you want to accomplish personally and the other for professional tasks and goals. Put a time frame on these items, taking into account some of your long-term goals. Next try to prioritize the two lists into one and look at the result. If it's skewed dramatically toward one side or the other—personal or professional—then you have no balance or very little balance at best.

For everything that's professional in life, you need something that's important personally. When you really examine what you do and why you do it, the personal things in your life are going to be the things that begin to take priority. Now is the time to start achieving and restoring balance to your life. Acknowledge the need for better balance and do something about it. Without balance, everything takes on the same importance, and when that happens, there are no priorities. Gaining balance will make you recognize and appreciate your total value, not only to your profession but to those in your personal life. In the final analysis, they are the most important things in your life.

Final Thought

The quality of balance determines job satisfaction.
Help your team establish and maintain balance.

 **Achieving Balance**

This worksheet will enable you to prioritize what you do and to start developing the balance and time management that will help you win every day.

Task and Time Required

1. _____

2. _____

3. _____

4. _____

5. _____

6. _____

7. _____

8. _____

9. _____

10. _____

Have I Included?

1. Time for me
2. Time for family
3. Time to evaluate
4. Time to plan (to visualize and to anticipate)
5. Plans that are consistent with weekly goals
6. High probability of success items at appropriate times
7. Toughest items when I am sharpest
8. Time for telephone calls
9. Tomorrow's planning
10. _____

Help Your Team to Achieve Balance

Chapter 15

Summary for Leaders

Winning versus Surviving

Winners are made, not born. An old cliché that applies here is simply that you can win if you're willing to pay the price. This is true in most cases.

When we talk about winners versus survivors, it's very easy until we begin to discuss those things that separate the winners from the survivors. Very often the winners do little things to push themselves over the top, things that we may not see until a game is over, the day is over, or the task is over. In business, the true winners not only talk the game but execute the winning ways. Winning can be contagious if it's given a chance.

As a leader, it's your responsibility to structure the environment so that winning is given a chance every day. It's often the case that winning deals or projects calls for the interaction of several departments in the workforce. Winning can be attached to a very simple task such as being able to walk across the room or even making a bed if you have a chronic illness. If, at the end of the day, you know that you did everything you possibly could to make progress on a task, you can feel like a winner, regardless of the outcome.

In your life, the quality of your interactions and the fine-tuning of the environment are crucial to winning consistently. Every player has a role on your team—and often people have more than one in order for the team to win. As we discussed in Chapter 6, selecting the appropriate players to help you win is crucial.

A quick review of the following winning habits whenever the feeling begins to wane will help you and your team sustain a higher level of performance. Don't misunderstand this list. The items listed are not sports factors that deal with winning. They are life factors that can fuel your everyday success.

Number 1: Winners expect to win every day, and that bucks the system. This is true of true leaders as well. We've talked about the fact that children are told approximately 200,000 times by the time they are 18 years old what *not* to do, therefore they come out into the world assuming that if they avoid failure, that winning will be a natural outcome, which, as we know, is not true. Your plan as a leader should be based on what you expect to gain instead of what you expect to avoid. Many times this posture, once it becomes habit, results in a major attitudinal upheaval and, most importantly, this attitude of expecting to achieve something every day puts the probability of success on your side for whatever you may be trying to accomplish.

Number 2: Winners have a positive mental attitude. I always tell people that they shouldn't feel good for no reason because it doesn't last very long. Instead, they should adopt a positive mental attitude because they're good at something. In other words, you need a positive mental attitude in your life in order to have positive expectations, but at the same time you need reinforcement to consistently support that positivity. In practice, this means you may have to back up on occasion and accomplish smaller, separate tasks to regain that positive attitude. Don't get bogged down by not being able to perform something that is very complex.

Number 3: Leaders play every day at as high an emotional level as they can control. From Chapter 12, which dealt with stretching your emotions every day, it should be obvious how important your emotional state is to winning. It's a part of winning. We should be proud of our emotions and willing to share them with other people. People become emotionally fatigued when they constantly relax and recover, so it's to your advantage to maintain a high level of emotion every day in whatever you're trying to accomplish. If you go over the edge emotionally, you have something in your mental bag to get you back to the edge (Chapter 12). If you're able to sustain a higher level of emotion, you don't suffer from the fatigue of having to recover back to the edge so many times on a given day.

Number 4: Leaders thrive on stress. We focused on this in Chapter 11 in our discussion of stress and anxiety. Stress can be a wonderful thing if you control the stressors. Just to review, 80 percent of stress is probably neither good nor bad when it comes to your physiological systems. We make stress negative through our reactions to it. The key is to focus your energy, which has traditionally been spent on battling stress, on using stress as an incentive to become better. Leaders are what you call the true tension seekers. In my case, being an MS patient, I have a lot of stress in my life, so every day I try to use those stressors to enable me to accomplish things that, at the start of the day, I may not have thought I could do. Even though I'm not able to accomplish everything, I'm at least able to do some things because I perceive stress as being an asset as opposed to a liability.

Number 5: Leaders have specific goals. We've talked many times about the importance of setting goals and the fact that doing the best you can is an easy way out but certainly not a beneficial way to approach every day. Winners always know exactly what they want to achieve within a specific time frame. As discussed in Chapter 4, goals need to be specific, difficult, and attainable so that at the end of the day when you accomplish what you had set out to, then you are able to reward yourself. Rewards give you recognition for all the things you did in a given day but they also take you to the next level with positive expectations.

Number 6: Leaders realize the importance of teamwork. Chapter 6 is devoted to assembling your team to include the folks who not only supplement your assets but also those who can counteract your liabilities. It's important that every player know his or her role on the team and be able to execute it. Good, open, honest communication with all the players on your team is the only way to facilitate this.

Number 7: Leaders communicate *with* team members, not *to* team members. There's an old cliché worth repeating here that what you are speaks so loudly people can't hear what you say. Very simply that means that your body language as well as what you say sends a strong message. These verbal and nonverbal means of communicating must be used in a very positive and constructive way so that every contact is truly a conversation and not a one-sided instructional time.

Number 8: In winning environments, leadership is tolerant of mistakes made while trying to succeed. If you don't make mistakes, then you're probably not accomplishing much because you're not taking risks. A certain amount of trial-and-error learning is significantly beneficial in the achievement of whatever skill it might be that you're trying to accomplish. There is nothing more harmful to development than creating an error-free environment where people are not permitted to face adversity and learn to recover from it. A very simple rule to follow if you're going to make a mistake is to make it trying to move forward. Don't make mistakes by moving away from something. This ensures that your energy is spent in trying to get better.

Number 9: Leaders must provide players with a winning environment. In other words, you need to be in an environment that motivates you. That is far more important than being surrounded by people who are trying to urge you on. Trying to motivate people is wasted energy that delivers only short-term results. But creating a motivating environment—by, for example, changing the wall colors, the furniture, the lighting, the pictures—has an impact on motivation. For 80 years studies have consistently shown that a change in environment that indicates an organization cares about its people causes an improvement in productivity. This is true not only in the business environment but also in sports and at home. To support people who have disabilities, team members can change things around, paint the walls, and help make the environment better and more comfortable. The effect is that you're going to be better at your job and much more productive in the environment.

Number 10: Leaders hold their focus and are able to change it quickly. We talked before about how important it is to develop a plan, but we also talked about the fact that it has to be flexible. No environment—no plan—is perfect, so there has to be a plan B. In many cases there are a number of different ways to accomplish the same goal. The focus of a good plan is the present and the future; it doesn't work to avoid past mistakes. Having a focus within your plan keeps you on track emotionally so that you don't veer and spend a lot of energy recovering.

Number 11: When focus is lost, winners are able to recover quickly, and leaders are able to help their team do the same. Now we just talked about the importance of having a focus and plan, but many times there are things that happen during your performance that don't always go according to plan. For example, heat can be detrimental to performance for people who have disabilities. Perhaps a person will have difficulty managing stress and the plan will be sent off track. Other times there are distractions or unexpected things in the environment that interrupt the plan. Those things are a part of real life and will happen. The basic goal is to get back to the plan as soon as possible, so there needs to be a clear recovery process in place. We've talked many times about the fact that recovery is not the issue. Everyone can recover; it's how quickly it happens that is the distinguishing factor for winners. So you need to develop in your mental bag things that will enable you to recover and return to the plan much more quickly.

Number 12: Leaders reward themselves. I mentioned previously that when you achieve goals and move in the direction of a positive outcome, you should reward yourself for your accomplishments and also your efforts. Small rewards for achieving steps toward longer-term goals are critical. It's not the reward itself. Self-reward is a legitimate vehicle for sustaining motivation, but it's not the ultimate goal.

Last year an award was given on a national women's fast-pitch softball team. In fact, two were given for each game. One winner was selected by the players, and the other was chosen by the coach. The reward was a penny. It was incredible how positively the players reacted to that penny. The concept and recognition were more important than the reward. Over the years there have been many coaches, especially in college swimming, who have used daily rewards. The top university for developing swimmers in the United States gave a single M&M candy as a reward for swimming a good practice lap. The M&M meant the world to the swimmers. People are not motivated by the material gain, but rather by the recognition for what they've done.

Number 13: Winning environments are not havens for survivors. With an increased emphasis, especially in the corporate environment, on getting more from fewer people, traditional survivors must begin to develop a taste for winning. In other words, as a company gets better and moves to a higher level, those folks who were merely survivors previously are going to be left behind. People who are complacent are not going to be able to stay in that work environment. Many times there are teams where a great player may have to be replaced because he or she no longer fits the chemistry of the team. In that particular environment, the person has abandoned winning and become a survivor. It doesn't mean someone is a bad person. It means people like that need to be in an environment where they are motivated to win and have more emphasis on their personal performance. It's very important that you as a leader constantly evaluate your teams, both on the personal and professional sides, in order to keep them strong. You may need to make changes periodically to keep a team strong because, as your team gets weaker, so do you. In keeping with the philosophy put forth in this book, all we need to do is get the clutter out of our minds and have people around us who can help us do that, move ahead, and accomplish something every day. You have to have a strong team around you every day in order to succeed.

Number 14: Leaders win because players want them to. On the surface it may not make much sense, but it's true. Good leaders are those who put the players in a position in which they can look good and play well. You must have, as a team, a burning desire to help each other. A leader many times sets the tone for that attitude. If you have a leader who's working with you, it's very important that he or she knows what motivates you, what your expectations are, what your environmental needs are, and what your training needs are so

Summary for Leaders

that you can perform better—and it's best if the leader hears it from you directly. I think everybody can use good coaching and good leadership. To me, overcoaching as a leader is worse than no coaching at all because it encourages your teammates to become coach-conscious players. That means they are always conscious that they're being watched. If they make a mistake, they look at the leader. If they don't perform well over time, they look at the leader. If something's wrong on the team, they look at the leader. Their productivity is hindered because half of their energy is spent looking for the leader's approval or intervention.

If you have a disability, your challenges are strong enough that you don't need the added burden of having someone around to make you coach conscious. As I've said before, leaders are good if they let their team play.

Number 15: Leaders have balance, as we explored in Chapter 14. It is a topic that is not discussed as much as it should be in seminars and in company environments. Consistent leaders recognize the importance of fulfillment, both personally and professionally, and they evaluate balance in terms of quality, not quantity, of time spent. There are so many corporate executives that I've worked with over the years who have no balance in their lives. If you look from the outside in at their accomplishments, your first thought is that they're very successful winners. But when you more fully understand their lives, you find that their personal lives are in a shambles and, despite their professional success, to me, they are undoubtedly losers in their overall lives. Unless you win both personally and professionally in your life, then you cannot claim to be a winner. If material gain is the most important thing in your life, then you're a very superficial person. If you have balance in your life, you realize that everything you do professionally is because of something that you want to support personally, not because you want to make more money for the sake of your bank account. There is no substitute for family; no friendships will be as strong as family. People who work 13, 14, or 15 hours a day are stealing time from the very side of life that gives you a reason to do your job. Workaholics who log long hours at work are likely to wake up one day and hate their jobs because they've stolen the things that were important to their personal lives. Balance is a real key that many times is disregarded in the corporate environment.

Number 16: Winners never apologize for being good. When I talk with multiple sclerosis (MS) patients, I tell them to never apologize for being well. If you could walk three miles, be proud to talk about it. If you can ride a mountain bike, don't think that you should feel bad about that because others with your condition cannot accomplish those things. Many times I think we're too humble, so we lose some of our self-confidence and self-esteem. When this happens, we feel like we do not deserve what we're getting out of life. Most of the time you'll find that people who are successful and accomplish certain things in life are able to succeed because they have a history of hard work, training, and commitment. Never apologize for being good at what you do.

Number 17: Leaders are totally committed to winning; in other words, they have a burning desire to do so. They use all their assets in an effort to accomplish something every single day, and they never let their liabilities roll over their strengths. Leaders build their lives around the things that they can accomplish, and eventually they are able to eliminate some of their liabilities. This is especially true for those of us with disabilities. If we thought more about the things we can accomplish and less about the things that drive us nuts, then we would be able to do more and we'd feel better about who we are. Every day, you have to have pride in who you are and what you bring to the party.

This chapter encompasses the key concepts of the whole book. If you're totally committed to doing things you haven't been able to do in the past, getting the clutter out of your life, and moving ahead, then you're going to realize a pride that surpasses anything you have felt previously. You're going to feel better about who you are and what you want to do—and it's going to be a fun ride from this day forward.

Final Thought

*Put your commonsense leadership style together
and have fun as a team-oriented leader.*

 **Your Pledge to Your Team**

Put all the concepts of this book together to create a realistic, attainable, and commonsense pledge to the team you lead.

_____

_____

_____

_____

_____

_____

_____

Index

C

Cattell 16. *See* 16 Personality Factor Questionnaire (16PF)

Cattell, Raymond, 32

Change
  to achieve balance, 195
  in assets/liabilities, 18
  behavior, 34, 42
  benefits of, 80–81
  commitment to, 55
  difficulty of, 80
  disgruntled workers, 53
  dramatic, 81
  environmental, 104
  via mental practice, 127
  visualization, 127, 129

Chemistry
  function of, 82
  overview of, 4–5
  talking about, 82–83

Childhood
  balance in, 190
  creativity in, 100–102
  critical learning period in, 137

Coaching
  consummate, 83
  experience and, 1
  leadership *vs.*, 10–11

Commonsense pledge, 213

Communication
  face-to-face, 85
  goals, 56–58
  with management, 97
  nonverbal, 23, 85

perceptual skills and, 115
  with team members, 206

Conservatives, 40

Controllable factors, 197–199

Core personality, 34

Corporate environment. *See also* Positive work environment
  adversary recovery in, 184
  assets and liabilities in, 18
  chemistry in, 4–5, 82–83
  culture of, 96–97
  enhancement of, 94
  excitement potential of, 71
  hours spent in, 193–195
  leadership in, 68–69
  manipulation of, 100–101
  modification of, 98–99
  motivation in, 136, 139
  multitasking in, 137–138
  perceptual development in, 114
  positive, enhancement exercise for, 105
  psychological noise in, 94–95
  stress in, 151
  structuring of, 203
  teamwork and, 86
  technology free, 102
  tolerance in, 206–207

Cox, Bobby, 83–84

Creativity
  in childhood, 100–102
  commonsense as, 101
  success and, 100–101

Critical learning period, 36–37

Self-reliance personality, 38–39
Senior citizens, 102–103, 116
Seven Habits of Highly Effective People, The (Covey), 107
Shepherd Spinal Center, 84
Shyness, 38
16 Personality Factor Questionnaire (16PF)
    components of, 36–41
    development of, 32
    scoring system of, 35
Smoltz, John, 158
Sober personality, 37–38
Source traits, 33–34
Stewart, Tony, 86, 185
Stress
    acceptance of, 151, 159
    appropriate challenging of, 158
    definition of, 148
    fun side of, 158
    health impacts of, 155
    impact of, 147–148
    multitasking and, 151
    overmanaging and, 153–154
    perception of, 148–149
    as positive incentive, 150
    relief from, 154–155, 154–158
    thriving on, 205
Stress management. *See also* Relaxation
    enhancement exercise for, 160–162
    laughter for, 158
    negative, 152–154

    positive, 155–158
Stressors
    changing to incentives, 157
    common, 149–150
    listings of, 156–157
    physical, 148–149
Success
    creativity and, 100–101
    fear of, 173–174
    mindset for, 68
    personality traits for, 5–6, 116–117
    visualization of, 184–185
Support meetings, 139
Surface traits, 33
Suspiciousness, 39

T
Teachable moments, 137
Teams. *See also* Workforce
    changes on, 80–81
    chemistry of, 4–5
    commitment to, 87
    communicating with, 85–86, 206
    contributions, recognition of, 81
    expectations of, 65
    formation of, 79–80
    goals of, 49–50
    good performance by, 96–97
    key function of, 79
    knowledge, enhancement exercise for, 91–92
    needs of, understanding, 141
    sharing among, 18–19